Audrey Hepburn

Audrey Hepburn

Michael Heatley

CHARTWELL
BOOKS

Brimming with creative inspiration, how-to projects, and useful information to enrich your everyday life, Quarto Knows is a favorite destination for those pursuing their interests and passions. Visit our site and dig deeper with our books into your area of interest: Quarto Creates, Quarto Cooks, Quarto Homes, Quarto Lives, Quarto Drives, Quarto Explores, Quarto Gifts, or Quarto Kids.

This edition published in 2017 by
CHARTWELL BOOKS
an imprint of The Quarto Group
142 West 36th Street, 4th Floor
New York, NY 10018 USA
www.QuartoKnows.com

© 2017 by Greene Media Ltd.

ISBN-13: 978-0-7858-3534-9

Printed and bound in China

10 9 8 7 6 5 4 3 2 1

Design: Greene Media Ltd

Any Internet site information provided was correct when provided by the Authors. The Publisher can accept no responsibility for this information becoming incorrect.

MIX
Paper from responsible sources
FSC® C101537

FRONT COVER and RIGHT: *Bettmann/Getty Images*

ABOVE: Sheet music cover for the song "Moon River" as used in the film *Breakfast at Tiffany's* sung by Audrey Hepburn. *GAB Archive/ Redferns/Getty Images*

PAGE 1: Audrey Hepburn waves at the camera; a 1950s' view. *Bob Thomas/Popperfoto/Getty Images*

PAGE 2: Audrey with her Yorkshire terrier Mr. Famous. *John Springer Collection/Corbis*

CONTENTS

INTRODUCTION

"Audrey is a magical combination of high chic and high spirits." Gregory Peck

When people hear the name Audrey Hepburn they immediately think of era-defining films and a fashion icon admired by generations. Epitomizing class and dignity, the Belgian-born British actress who made her name in Hollywood was seen as the benchmark of style in the 1950s and 1960s—a true star of the silver screen.

It's nearly two decades since Audrey Hepburn took her final bow, but still her image and legacy continue to bewitch the world. Given that she would now be in her eighties were she still with us, it's a fair bet that many of her fans weren't even born when she first set foot on the world stage. That was on Broadway in 1951, and within three years she was carrying off her first Tony Award, the stage equivalent of the Oscar. Bigger things clearly beckoned.

Hollywood inevitably came calling, and it was the big screen on which the girl born Audrey Kathleen Ruston would create her mystique. Starring opposite a roll call of the era's most eligible leading men, she became one of the most successful and popular actresses in the world. By the mid-1960s, any director seeking her services would be looking at writing seven figures in his dollar chequebook.

Yet at the height of her fame Hepburn took time out to spend time with her family. Not a move today's fame-hungry stars would contemplate, and even in 1969 her decision raised eyebrows. Yet it was always going to be an au revoir rather than a farewell, and the middle of the 1970s saw her resume her career in the public eye.

Even then, many of her fans were unaware of the problems and prejudices Audrey had been subjected to in her pre-fame life. She'd been born in Belgium between the wars, and her parents had divorced when she was still very young. She would refer to her father's abandonment of the family as the most traumatic moment of her life.

She, her mother and two half-brothers lived in occupied Holland during the war and she had to develop her acting skills to avoid detection by the authorities: half-brother Ian was not so lucky. Much of what she saw in the war years awoke Audrey to the darker side of life. This was one reason why family was so important to her, not to mention humanitarian causes.

RIGHT: The cocktail dress worn by Audrey in *Breakfast at Tiffany's* on display during a preview of an auction at Christie's, New York, May 24, 2007. It sold for $192,000. *Shannon Stapleton/Reuters/Corbis*

But those who remember Hepburn's Holly Golightly in 1961's *Breakfast at Tiffany's* need not appreciate these facts. This iconic character topped off a rise that had begun with 1953's *Roman Holiday*, a movie where she beat Elizabeth Taylor to secure the female lead. To win an Oscar with your first starring role was unusual, but then Audrey Hepburn was no ordinary girl.

The year before she left the screen for the final time in 1989 she had committed herself to work for UNICEF in some of the world's most underprivileged areas. Sadly, Audrey Hepburn's career as a full-time humanitarian was cut short, and she died in 1993. But she remains today as iconic as ever. In 1999 the American Film Institute rated her the third greatest female film star of all time, beaten only by (the unrelated) Katharine Hepburn and Bette Davis. This is the Audrey Hepburn story in words and pictures. The icon, and the inspiration, lives on …

LEFT: Humphrey Bogart said of her, "With Audrey it's kind of unpredictable. She's like a good tennis player—she varies her shots." *Bettmann/Corbis*

RIGHT: "Jewelry just doesn't suit me, and if I wear too much makeup, my face looks like a mask instead of me … Put me in furs and jewels, and I look like something off a barrel organ." Audrey in *Sabrina*. *Underwood & Underwood/Corbis*

TIMELINE

1929

May 4—Audrey Kathleen van Heemstra Ruston is born on Rue Keyenveld in Ixelles, Brussels, Belgium.

June—Audrey stops breathing during a bad case of whooping cough. Her mother revives her with "a little spanking and a lot of faith."

1932

January—the family moves to Linkebeek, a nearby Brussels municipality.

1935

Audrey's father walks out.

May 14—Audrey starts at boarding school in England: Miss Rigden's School, Elham, Kent.

1938

Audrey's parents' divorce comes through.

1939

The family moves to Arnhem in neutral Holland.

1940

May 10—Germany attacks the Netherlands. A week later the country is in the hands of the Nazis.

1941

Audrey begins her first serious ballet training under Winja Marova at the Arnhem School of Music.

1942

Audrey's brother Ian is sent to work in a munitions factory in Berlin. Audrey and her mother move in with Baron van Heemstra in Velp.

1944

September 17—Operation Market Garden starts with major Allied paratroop drops. Its failure condemns Arnhem to a further winter of Nazi occupation.

1945

May 4—The Netherlands are liberated on Audrey's sixteenth birthday.

Audrey studies in Amsterdam at The Balletstudio 45 with Sonia Gaskell, the leading name in Dutch ballet.

1946

Audrey dances in a matinee performance at Amsterdam's Hortus theater.

1948

Audrey auditions for Marie Rambert ballet school. She wins a partial scholarship.

Audrey's first film role—as a stewardess in *Nederlands in Zeven Lessen* (Dutch in Seven Lessons).

Audrey leaves Amsterdam for London and the Ballet Rambert.

Audrey auditions for and gets a job in the chorus line of *High Button Shoes*. Her one line is, "Have they all gone?"

December 22—*High Button Shoes* starts at the London Hippodrome and runs for 291 performances.

1949
Audrey is cast in *Sauce Tartare*, which opens at the Cambridge Theatre. After 433 performances the play is refreshed as *Sauce Piquante*.

Audrey takes elocution lessons from actor Felix Aylmer.

1950
Audrey plays a cigarette girl in the film *Laughter in Paradise*, released on June 13, 1951.

1951
Audrey gets a major role in T*he Secret People* (released 1952). While shooting she gets a role in *Monte Carlo Baby* (shot simultaneously in French as *Nous Irons à Monte Carlo*), on location on the French Riviera. During her time in France, Colette sees Audrey in a hotel lobby and decides she looks perfect for the lead role in *Gigi*.

Audrey performs in four other films released this year: *Laughter in Paradise, One Wild Oat, Young Wives' Tale*, and *The Lavender Hill Mob*.

September 18—Audrey's screen test at Pinewood Studios for the role of Princess Ann in William Wyler's *Roman Holiday* lands her first Hollywood movie, a salary of $12,500 and an option for a second Paramount picture.

October—*Gigi* rehearsals begin.

November—Audrey appears in Vogue for the first time (photographed by Irving Penn).

November 24—*Gigi* opens at the Fulton Theatre and runs for 219 performances. Audrey wins the 1952 Theatre World Award for her performance.

December 4—announcement in *The Times*: Mr J.E. Hanson and Miss A. Hepburn: The engagement is announced between James, son of Mr and Mrs Robert Hanson, of Norwood Grange, Huddersfield, Yorkshire, and Audrey Hepburn, daughter of Baroness Ella van Heemstra, of 65 South Audley St, London, W1.

1952
May 31—*Gigi* closes in New York and Audrey goes straight to Rome to shoot *Roman Holiday*. During filming she begins her collaboration and friendship with Edith Head.

Wedding plans are put off again as Audrey goes from *Roman Holiday* into the American road tour of *Gigi*, that lasts eight months. Midway, Audrey announces her engagement to Hanson is over. On her return to London after the *Gigi* tour she meets Gregory Peck's friend Mel Ferrer, who later sends her the script for *Ondine*.

ABOVE: Edith Head designed the ivory lace gown Audrey wore in *Roman Holiday*; it was then modified and she wore it to pick up her Oscar. Here displayed at the Kerry Taylor auction house in London. This dress will later sell at auction in 2011 for £84,000. *EPA/Kerim Okten/Corbis*

1953

August 27—*Roman Holiday* premieres in New York City. It goes on to win Audrey the 1953 Best Actress award from the New York Film Critics Circle, as well as a BAFTA, a Golden Globe, and an Oscar. Edith Head won an Oscar for Best Black and White Costume.

September—Audrey appears on the cover of *TIME* magazine.

September—shooting for *Sabrina* starts on Long Island. The nine-week shoot is followed by time in Hollywood for retakes. Edith Head wins an Oscar for costume design but Hubert de Givenchy designs most of Audrey's costumes and starts a lifelong relationship.

December—rehearsals for *Ondine* start. Audrey plays a water nymph, a role for which she will receive the 1954 Best Actress Tony.

1954

February 18—*Ondine* premieres at New York's 46th Street Theatre.

March 25—Audrey is awarded the 1953 Best Actress Oscar.

March 28—Audrey receives her Tony for best stage actress for *Ondine*.

July 3—*Ondine* closes after 157 performances. Audrey, on medical advice, flies to a clinic in Switzerland. After a week she moves to a villa below the Bürgenstock mountain above Lake Lucerne.

August—Mel Ferrer flies to Bürgenstock and proposes.

September 24—Mel and Audrey are married in a civil ceremony at Buoche. The next day there is a religious ceremony at Bürgenstock.

November—Audrey returns to Holland for a fundraising tour at the invitation of the League of Dutch Military War Invalids.

1955

February—Audrey is nominated for an Oscar for *Sabrina*, but loses out to Grace Kelly in *The Country Girl*.

February 23—Audrey wins the Golden Globe for World Film Favorite – Female in 1955.

July 4—shooting begins on *War and Peace*. Her performance earns her $350,000, the highest ever for an actress at the time, and 1956 nominations for BAFTA and Golden Globe.

1956

April 9—shooting of *Funny Face* starts in Hollywood …

July 19—and ends following a month on location in Paris. Givenchy designs all of Audrey's clothes for the film.

August 21—*War and Peace* released to critical acclaim.

August 24—shooting starts on another Billy Wilder film, *Love in the Afternoon*.

December—Audrey leaves Europe to spend Christmas with Mel near Palm Springs.

1957

January—Audrey and Mel work on the television movie *Mayerling* at the NBC studios—her only film work of

ABOVE: Audrey and Mel Ferrer. *Mirrorpix*

1957. She chooses to reject movie offers for the rest of the year and accompanies Mel to Spain and Mexico for the shooting of *The Sun Also Rises* (which premieres on August 23).

February 13—*Funny Face* is released. Impressive as cast, score, and costumes are, the film is a box-office failure.

June 30—*Love in the Afternoon* is released. While it achieves reasonable critical reviews, it is again relatively unsuccessful at the box office. Audrey is nominated for a Golden Globe and a New York Film Critics Circle Award, but wins a Laurel Award from *Motion Picture Exhibitor* magazine.

1958
January 24—Filming for *The Nun's Story* begins in Rome and is followed by location work in the Belgian Congo.

July—Audrey sustains back injuries in a car accident and resolves never to drive again.

November—Audrey finishes work on *Green Mansions* directed by her husband. At Christmas she discovers she is pregnant.

1959
January 28—during filming of *The Unforgiven* Audrey is thrown by her horse and fractures four vertebrae. She will later miscarry and lose her baby.

May 19—*Green Mansions* is released and is panned ...

July 18—but all is forgotten when *The Nun's Story*, widely regarded as Audrey's finest work, is released. She wins the 1959 Best Actress BAFTA and is named Best Actress of 1959 by the New York Film Critics. She is also nominated for, but does not win, the Best Actress Oscar.

September 30—Audrey and Mel attend the dedication of Audrey Hepburnlaan (Audrey Hepburn Lane), in Doorn, Netherlands.

1960
Audrey refuses all work—including *West Side Story*—after discovering she is pregnant again. She accepts *Breakfast at Tiffany's* only if it can be started after the birth.

April 6—*The Unforgiven* is released to a lukewarm response.

July 17—Audrey gives birth to Sean. He is baptized in September in the same chapel where Audrey and Mel married.

ABOVE: Audrey reads a cover story about herself in a Japanese magazine, while relaxing on the set of *The Children's Hour*. Bettmann/ Corbis

October 2—*Breakfast at Tiffany's* starts shooting on the corner of 57th and Fifth in New York. For her iconic role, Audrey will be nominated for an Oscar but again not win.

1961

January 8—Audrey reads a poem at the Friars Club testimonial dinner for Gary Cooper in Hollywood.

March—*The Children's Hour* (in UK *The Loudest Whisper*) reunites Audrey with William Wyler. During the Hollywood shoot Audrey's dog, Mr. Famous, is run over on Wilshire Boulevard. Mel quickly assuages her grief by presenting her with a new dog, Sam.

October 5—*Breakfast at Tiffany's* released in New York

December 19—*The Children's Hour* released. *The New York Times* review says: "... it is not too well acted, except by Audrey Hepburn ..."

1962

July–November—*Paris When it Sizzles* is filmed pairing Audrey once more with William Holden. Afterwards, Audrey remains in Paris to film *Charade* with Cary Grant. Shooting ends in January 1963.

1963

May 29—Audrey sings "Happy Birthday, Mr. President" to JFK at the Waldorf Astoria.

August 13—*My Fair Lady* starts filming; it will be Audrey's most controversial film, but a huge success. She becomes only the third actor ever to receive $1 million for a movie.

December 5—*Charade* opens in New York: the quick-fire repartee between Cary Grant and Audrey ensures its success.

1964

April 8—*Paris When it Sizzles* finally opens.

October—*My Fair Lady* opens in New York (21st) and Los Angeles (28th). *The New York Times* enthuses: "Audrey Hepburn superbly justifies the decision of the producer, Jack L. Warner, to get her to play the title ... it is the brilliance of Miss Hepburn ... that gives an extra touch of subtle magic and individuality to the film."

1965

July—*How to Steal a Million* starts shooting, once again teaming Audrey and director William Wyler in Paris.

September—on completion of filming, the Ferrers buy La Paisible (peaceful/tranquil), an 18th-century farmhouse in Tolochenaz-sur-Morges.

1966

July—*How to Steal a Million* opens in LA (16th) and New York (17th). *The New York Times* reviewer (Bosley Crowther) says: "Cheers all around for everybody—for Miss Hepburn, Mr. O'Toole, Mr. Griffith, Eli Wallach ..."

May 3—shooting starts on *Two for the Road*, costarring Albert Finney, a young British actor who gave the film more of an edge than Audrey's usual aging male costars.

1967

January 19—filming starts on *Wait Until Dark*, with Mel as producer. Audrey plays a blind woman. She works so hard that she loses almost fifteen pounds while filming.

April 27—*Two for the Road* released. *The New York Times* critic Bosley Crowther savaged the film, but it was well-received in Europe. Director Stanley Donen considered this performance the best of Audrey's career.

September—Audrey and Mel file for divorce.

October 26—*Wait Until Dark* released in the U.S. The film is a great success, and Audrey's fifth (and final) Oscar nomination follows, as do nominations for Best Actress for the Golden Globe and New York Film Critics Circle.

Audrey will not make another film until 1976.

1968

June—Audrey meets Andrea Dotti, an Italian psychiatrist nine years her junior, on a private cruise.

November 21—the Ferrers' divorce is announced.

December 24—Dotti proposes and Audrey accepts.

1969

January 18—Audrey marries Dotti at Morges town hall.

1970

February 8—Luca Dotti is born by Caesarean section in Lausanne.

1971

Audrey is involved in a UNICEF TV special, hosted by Julie Andrews. Audrey, representing Italy, explains the legend of "La Befana."

Audrey earns £30,000 for work on four minute-long commercials for Japanese wig company Varie.

1975

May–July—*Robin and Marian* is filmed in Spain with director Dick Lester.

1976

March 11—*Robin and Marian* premieres at Radio City Music Hall. *Chicago Sun-Times* critic Roger Ebert said of Audrey and Sean Connery's performance: "They glow. They really do seem in love. And they project as marvelously complex, fond, tender people."

March 14—Audrey appears on TV paying tribute to

William Wyler as he becomes the fourth person to receive an American Film Institute's Lifetime award.

March 29—Audrey presents the Best Picture Oscar to producer Michael Douglas for *One Flew Over the Cuckoo's Nest*.

1978

Audrey attends the BAFTAs and presents Fred Zinnemann with his fellowship.

ABOVE: Hubert de Givenchy and Audrey Hepburn at the show celebrating Givenchy's 30th anniversary. *Bettmann/Corbis*

November—shooting starts on the Sidney Sheldon thriller *Bloodline* with costars Ben Gazzara and James Mason.

1979

June 29—*Bloodline* is released to critical reviews. On the promotional tour, reporters concentrate on questions about Dotti's indiscretions rather than the film.

November 23—Robert Wolders' wife, film star Merle Oberon, dies. Robert will meet Audrey for the first time at a dinner party arranged by Connie Wald.

1980

April–July—shooting for Peter Bogdanovich's comedy, *They All Laughed*, starts in Manhattan. Sean Ferrer is production assistant and has a small role. While in New York Audrey meets Robert Wolders again.

September—Vero Roberti, Andrea Dotti's stepfather, announces that Audrey's marriage has ended and she has filed for divorce.

1981

August 14—*They All Laughed opens*. Acclaimed at the Venice Film Festival, other reviews are more critical.

April 8—Robert accompanies Audrey to Los Angeles for the American Film Institute Tribute to Fred Astaire, shown on TV on the 18th. He will be at her side for the majority of her future outings, including the arduous UNICEF tours.

1982

May 10—Audrey attends the gala opening of "Givenchy – 30 Years," a retrospective exhibition at the New York's Fashion Institute of Technology.

The Dotti divorce is finalized

1983

Audrey hosts the Marie Rambert Memorial Gala at Sadler's Wells, London—Rambert died in 1982.

September 19—Audrey attends the tribute to Ingrid Bergman Gala, Venice, a year after her death from cancer.

1984

August 26—Baroness Ella van Heemstra dies at La Paisible at the age of eighty-four.

1985

Sean Ferrer marries Marina Spadafora; the relationship only lasts until 1989.

1986

Audrey is among those interviewed for *Directed by William Wyler*, a documentary tribute produced by Wyler's daughter.

1987

February 23—*Love Among Thieves*, a made for TV film, sees Audrey starring opposite Richard Wagner. It is her last starring role.

March 6—Sean Connery and Audrey are made Commanders Of The Arts And Letters, France's most prestigious award.

During 1987 Audrey undertakes a number of ad hoc missions for UNICEF including appearances in Japan and Macao.

1988

March 9—Audrey is appointed a UNICEF Special Ambassador and in 1989 a Goodwill Ambassador. She immediately undertakes a trip to Ethiopia (March 14–18)

ABOVE: Sean Connery and Audrey are made Commanders of the Arts And Letters March 6, 1987. *Patrick Robert/Sygma/Corbis*

and ends the year in Latin America (Venezuela and Ecuador).

From 1988 until 1992, Audrey and Roger Moore host the Danny Kaye International Children's Special in Holland.

November—Audrey stars in "Gift of Song" a televised concert from Vancouver benefitting the Canadian UNICEF Committee.

November 30—Audrey is presented with the first annual Winternight Award on behalf of Lighthouse, a New York association for the Blind.

1989

February—Audrey travels for UNICEF to Central America, and visits Honduras, El Salvador and Guatemala. She launches the 1989 *State of the World's Children Report*.

April—Audrey represents UNICEF in Washington, D.C. before the House Select Subcommittee on Hunger after which she travels to the Sudan.

May 15—filming starts for *Always*, with Steven Spielberg directing. Audrey provides a cameo performance as an angel.

October—Audrey travels for UNICEF to Australia,Thailand, and Bangladesh.

December 22—*Always* released, Audrey's last screen performance.

1990

January 20—Audrey is presented the special Cecil B. DeMille Award at the Golden Globes for her contribution to the entertainment industry.

Spring–Summer—filming takes place on *Gardens of the World* a PBS TV documentary, Audrey's final performances.

July—a tulip is named after Audrey. She and her Aunt Jacqueline attend a dedication ceremony at Huis Doorn in Apeldoorn, Holland.

November—Audrey travels to Australia for UNICEF, then Vietnam.

December—Audrey plays a major role through media interviews at the New York launch of the 1991 State of the

World's Children Report.

1991

March 8—Audrey hosts the PBS Special *The Fred Astaire Songbook*.

March—a one-hour-long *Gardens of the World* preview airs to acclaim.

April 22—Audrey is honored at the Film Society of Lincoln Center. Gregory Peck, Billy Wilder, and Ralph Lauren are among the stars honoring her for her life's work.

1992

Audrey Hepburn's Enchanted Tales is released. On the spoken-word album Audrey reads various classic children's stories. It earns her a posthumous Grammy Award for Best Spoken Word Album for Children

March 30—Audrey presents an honorary Oscar to Indian director Satyajit Ray at the Academy Awards ceremony.

September—Audrey travels to war-torn Somalia for UNICEF. During the trip she suffers from stomach pains.

November 1—Audrey undergoes testing at Cedars-Sinai Medical Center and is operated on. She returns home to Switzerland, with weeks to live.

December 11—President George Bush awards Audrey the highest civilian honor available, the Presidential Medal of Freedom, for her UNICEF work.

1993

January—Audrey is the recipient of the SAG Achievement Award accepted on her behalf at the ceremony by Julia Roberts.

January 20—Audrey dies at home in her sleep.

January 21—the first of eight episodes of *Gardens of the World* airs on PBS TV.

January 24—Audrey is buried in the cemetery at Tolochenaz-sur-Morges.

March 29—Audrey posthumously receives the Jean Hersholt Humanitarian Award at the Academy Awards.

September 18—Audrey wins a posthumous Emmy for Outstanding Individual Achievement – Informational Programming for *Gardens of the World*.

1994

The Audrey Hepburn Children's Fund is created by her sons, Sean and Luca, and long-time companion, Robert Wolders, in order to continue her work.

1999

June 15—the American Film Institute named Hepburn third among the Greatest Female Stars of All Time.

2000

March 27—a dramatization of Audrey's life entitled *The Audrey Hepburn Story* airs on TV.

2006

December 5—the "little black dress" from *Breakfast at Tiffany's*, designed by Givenchy, is sold at a Christie's auction for £467,200, the highest price paid for a dress from a film.

2007

September 30—Andrea Dotti dies from complications of a colonoscopy.

2008

June 2—Mel Ferrer dies of heart failure at the age of ninety.

2009

December 8—a London auction of Hepburn's film wardrobe raises £270,200. Half the auction's proceeds go to the Audrey Hepburn Children's Foundation and UNICEF.

2011

November 29—at the Kerry Taylor "Passion for Fashion" auction, Audrey's ivory lace gown from *Roman Holiday*—which she also used in modified form to collect her Oscar—raises £84,000.

BELOW: Sean H. Ferrer poses during the exhibition "Timeless Audrey" in Berlin, March 12, 2009. *Rainer Jensen/Corbis*

THE EARLY YEARS 1929–47

"I have often thought of myself as quite ugly. In fact, I used to have quite a complex about it. To be frank, I've often been depressed and deeply disappointed in myself. You can even say that I hated myself at certain periods. I was too fat, or maybe too tall, or just plain too ugly. I couldn't seem to handle any of my problems or cope with people I met. If you want to get psychological, you can say my definiteness stems from underlying feelings of insecurity and inferiority. I couldn't conquer these feelings by acting indecisive. I found the only way to get the better of them was ... by adopting a forceful, concentrated drive."
Audrey Hepburn

Audrey Kathleen Ruston was born to Joseph Victor Anthony Ruston and Ella van Heemstra in the municipality of Ixelles in the Brussels region of Belgium on May 4, 1929. She was of good stock; her mother was from Dutch nobility and a former Baroness, while her lineage also combined Czech, Austrian and French ancestry.

Both Audrey's parents, who wed in 1926, had been married before. Audrey had two stepbrothers, Alexander and Ian, from Ella's previous marriage. The surname Hepburn was that of her paternal grandmother, and would not be added until later.

A severe case of whooping cough threatened to end the Audrey Hepburn story at just three weeks old; she was only revived by her mother spanking her after her heart stopped. She would endure and survive further adversity before her childhood was over.

An introverted child, her mother sent her to boarding school in Kent aged five. It was here she got an early taste of independence in a country she would spend a large part of her life. It was also here she began her lifelong love of ballet.

But her life was soon to undergo an abrupt change when father Joseph, a fascist with anti-Semitic views, abandoned the family in May 1935. Audrey was devastated: "[It was] the most traumatic event of my life—a tragedy from which I don't think I've ever recovered. I worshipped him and missed him terribly since the day he disappeared."

Ella received custody of Audrey, but Joseph demanded

ABOVE: Allied paratroops and gliders land near Arnhem during Operation "Market," the air component of Operation "Market Garden," September 1944. *Popperfoto/Getty Images*

ABOVE: Home of Audrey's grandfather, Aarnoud Baron van Heemstra (1871–1957), who was mayor of Arnhem 1910–20, and whom she often visited. When the family moved from Belgium to Arnhem in September 1939, they stayed here to begin with. *Casper Kuijer*

ABOVE RIGHT: Audrey, her mother, and her two half-brothers, Alexander and Ian, moved to Sickeszlaan 7, near Park Sonsbeek, in which they would live for three months. *Casper Kuijer*

RIGHT: Mel Ferrer and Audrey admire the unveiling of a street named in her honor at Doorn, Holland, October 6, 1959. *Bettmann/ Corbis*

she stay in England; he received visitation rights, which he did not exercise. On the outbreak of war her mother believed she would be safer in neutral Holland than in London. It would be the last time she saw her father for nearly twenty years.

Back in the eastern Dutch municipality of Arnhem, Ella feared her daughter's name could be detrimental to their safety and changed into the less English-sounding Edda van Heemstra. It made no difference to Audrey, who had more than an identity crisis to surmount. No more Dutch than English, she found herself isolated at school and was forced to learn the language quickly.

Her ambition to become a ballerina was nurtured during lessons at the Arnhem Conservatory. But when the Germans took charge of the town in 1940, lessons were not the only thing that was disrupted. The occupation hit available resources, and everyday life became a trial: soon enough Audrey and her mother were soon suffering from malnutrition and the freezing winter conditions. She attempted to keep her spirits up by immersing herself in dance, performing in secret and continuing to hone her skills until too weak to do so from lack of food.

At the same time, unknown to Audrey or her mother, father Joseph Ruston had been imprisoned in England for being a fascist sympathiser, first in London and later on the Isle of Man. Audrey, for her part, witnessed Jewish families being placed in cattle trucks en route to Nazi concentration camps. "I was eleven or so, and all the nightmares I've ever had are mingled with that," she later recalled. Her half-brother Ian was sent to work in a factory in Berlin, his family unaware of his fate. As well as overcoming the absence of her father, this was yet another burden for the youngster to bear.

The German occupation lasted five years, and Audrey later reflected in a 1956 interview that she might well not have made it: "Had we known we were going to be occupied for five years, we might have all shot ourselves. We though it would be over next week … six months …

next year … that's how we got through."

The war ended and Arnhem was eventually liberated in 1945, albeit in a protracted and bloody fashion. But while the violence had finally ended, the mental and emotional scars inflicted on the innocent civilians continued and would have a profound affect on the rest of Audrey's life.

In March 1988 she said of this time: "I was in Holland during the war, during the German occupation, and food dwindled. The last winter was the worst of all. By then, food was scarce, and whatever there was went to the troops. There's a big difference between dying of starvation and malnutrition, of course, but I was very, very under-nourished. Immediately after the war, an organization, which later became UNICEF, instantly came in with the Red Cross and brought relief for the people in the form of food, medication and clothes. All the local schools were turned into relief centers. I was one of the beneficiaries with the other children. I've known about UNICEF all my life."

Mother and daughter's next stop was Amsterdam, where they continued rebuilding their life after the war. She continued dancing, this time for leading Dutch dance icon—and Lithuanian Jew—Sonia Gaskell. Her school, which had emerged from hiding after the occupation,

ABOVE LEFT: Arnhem's Stadsschouwburg (city theater) opened in 1938. On May 9, 1940, the day before the German invasion of The Netherlands, Audrey attended a ballet performance there by the Sadler's Wells Ballet company, with prima ballerina Margot Fonteyn. Audrey presented a bouquet of flowers at the end of the performance to the director of the company. On January 8, 1944, her ballet school held a performance here. *Casper Kuijer*

ABOVE: This bust of Audrey Hepburn by artist Kees Verkade was unveiled on April 23, 1994, by Dutch comedian and fellow UNICEF Goodwill Ambassador Paul van Vliet. *Casper Kuijer*

LEFT: A pupil lifts 68-year old Marie Rambert, head of the Rambert Ballet. *Hulton-Deutsch Collection/Corbis*

would later become the Netherlands Ballet. Audrey's place was a testament to her natural talent, though her largely self-taught technique was slightly awkward.

She remained there for three years while many around her were discussing the opportunities for dancers in England—specifically London. With a British father and passport, Audrey had the chance to head to the United Kingdom, and took it.

She auditioned for esteemed Polish teacher Marie Rambert's ballet school and was accepted with a scholarship. The next chapter of Audrey Hepburn's career was about to begin, but she had no clue what a different direction life would take in London.

AUDREY AND ELLA

"My mother desperately wanted to become an actress. Yet my grandfather strictly forbade her to go near the stage. He was adamant. He felt the occupation was beneath his daughter, and might reflect badly on the Van Heemstra heritage. I don't think my mother ever got over her disappointment in obeying him." Audrey Hepburn

The closest, longest and most unquestioned relationship of Audrey's life was with her mother, Baroness Ella van Heemstra, who was born in Velp on June 12, 1900. She was one of nine children of Baron Arnoud Jan Adolf van Heemstra, who had been the governor of Dutch Guiana in South America, and Baroness Elbrig Wilhelmine Henrietta van Asbeck. Ella grew up in privileged circumstances, but like Audrey was unlucky in her choice of husbands. She had two sons—Ian and Alexander—by her first marriage and Audrey by her second, to John Victor Hepburn-Ruston, an Anglo-Irish banker who deserted the family in 1935.

Ella was not the most demonstrative of mothers and Audrey said of her, "She was not the most affectionate person—in fact there were times when I thought she was cold—but she loved me in her heart, and I knew that all along." Evidence of this, if any were needed, is provided in a remarkable story told by Michael Burn, a British commando captured at St. Nazaire and imprisoned in Colditz, who met Ella and Audrey in England before the war. When Burn was in his first prison camp he received a Red Cross parcel and only learned who it came from after the war. Ella recognized Burn in a Nazi newsreel in Holland and, with the help of the Jewish owner of the cinema, cut out a frame from the film and contacted the Red Cross. In return, Burn was able to respond to Ella's pleas in the awful days after the war when Audrey was at death's door from an infection brought on by malnutrition. Burn sent Ella cartons of cigarettes which she sold on the black market and thereby raised enough money to buy penicillin to save her daughter's life.

Ella went to London with Audrey and took on menial jobs, including cleaning, to support them while Audrey was with the Ballet Rambert. She was at Audrey's side when she won her Oscar, and she frequently accompanied her daughter on film shoots, even making a brief appearance as a lady sitting outside a café in the film *Funny Face*.

Ella did not approve of Audrey's choice of husbands, although she did like Robert Wolders.

Known to Audrey's family as "Tante Ella," she moved to La Paisible in her later years and died there on August 26, 1984. "I was lost without my mother," said Audrey. "She had been my sounding board, my conscience."

RIGHT: Ella and Audrey in 1946. *Hulton Archive/Getty Images*

2

FROM LONDON
TO BROADWAY 1948-52

"I was born with an enormous need for affection and a terrible need to give it. That's what I'd like to think maybe has been the appeal. People have recognized something in me they have themselves—the need to receive affection and the need to give it." Audrey Hepburn

When Audrey and her mother left Amsterdam and headed to England in 1948, they traveled in the hope of realizing the potential of Audrey's blossoming ballet career. They were equally keen to leave the atrocities they had witnessed behind.

Circumstances had obliged the redoubtable Ella van Heemstra to assume the role of both father and mother and there is no doubt that she was an overbearing, fiercely protective character. Audrey would have a constant fight to emerge from her shadow.

Audrey began her education at the Rambert ballet school. Sadly, the consequences of her time in Arnhem, her malnourishment and other ailments suffered during the period—allied to her height—meant she would never reach the pinnacle of her profession and become a prima ballerina.

Undaunted, she briefly turned to modeling; the jobs made her comfortable in front of the camera, something she would make look easy for the rest of her career.

Audrey found a way to combine her modeling and dance training as she tried out for a role in the chorus line of *High Button Shoes*, a musical choreographed by Jerome Robbins, who would later go to work on *West Side Story* and *The King And I*.

Though her role was minor, it didn't stop the nerves: "I went tearing across [the stage] holding a girl by her hand and said, 'Have they all gone?' Believe me, I was nervous every single night. I used to repeat it to myself over and over before going on."

Though she only had one line, Audrey cruised through the audition process and it would be enough to get her noticed. She was cast in another musical, *Sauce Piquante*, in 1949 while improving her singing voice and continuing to model.

Working nearly seven days a week to support herself, Audrey's work was paying off slowly as she gained a few minor roles in motion pictures. Her first appearance was as a girl selling cigarettes in Associated British Pathé's *Laughter In Paradise*. She was offered a seven-year ABC contract as a result, but preferred to stay freelance for the time being.

Hepburn went on to work on an ABC film, *One Wild Oat*, starring Stanley Holloway, who would play Audrey's father thirteen years later in *My Fair Lady*. It was another bit-part role for now, though, as she portrayed a hotel receptionist.

The summer of 1951 saw Hepburn appear in Academy Award-winning comedy caper *The Lavender Hill Mob*.

Audrey and Babs Johnston (right) auditioning for a part as chorus girls in Jack Hylton's *High Button Shoes*, 1948. *Popperfoto/Getty Images*

This starred a young Alec Guinness, who would later go on to portray Obi Wan Kenobe in the *Star Wars* trilogy, alongside Stanley Holloway as two crooks involved in a bungled gold heist. Unfortunately Hepburn's cameo as Chiquita was all too brief at barely ten seconds long, but it would be one of her last minor roles.

Guinness, like many others at the time, was stunned by Hepburn's mesmerizing looks. "She only had half a line to say…but her faun-like beauty and presence were remarkable."

Next came *Monte Carlo Baby*, a comedy filmed in 1951 that wouldn't hit the screen until a year later. Hepburn was spotted at this time by novelist Sidonie-Gabrielle Colette who immediately picked her for the Broadway adaptation of her 1944 novel *Gigi*. Audrey Hepburn was beginning to be noticed.

February 1952 saw Hepburn's first star billing in a British film, *The Secret People*. She starred as Nora Brentano opposite Italian Valentina Cortese, who was

LEFT: American producer Archie Thompson conducting *High Button Shoes* auditions in London's West End. To Audrey's left is Eugenie Sivyer. *Popperfoto/Getty Images*

BELOW: Chorus girls from the show *Sauce Tartare*—L–R, Aud Johanssen, Audrey, and Enid Smeedon—relax on the roof of the Cambridge Theatre in London, June 28, 1949. *Ron Case/Keystone/Hulton Archive/Getty Images*

ABOVE: Audrey Hepburn takes a break from *Sauce Tartare* at the National Exhibition of Cage Birds. *Mirrorpix*

RIGHT: Audrey poses for the cameras near Elstree, July 1949. *Mirrorpix*

instrumental in getting Audrey the part. "I went to the director and said, 'if you really love me, I would like to have as the sister that little girl.' They said,'We were going to look at some others.' I said, 'No, I beg you—I want her.' " The film may have disappeared without trace, but Audrey was noticed: *Variety* said, "Audrey Hepburn, in a minor role as the kid sister, combines beauty with skill, shining particularly in two short dance sequences."

By this time Audrey was settled in England after her brief stay on Broadway and had found a partner in young entrepreneur James (later Lord) Hanson. The pair had met in 1949, shortly after Audrey had finished *The Lavender Hill Mob*. Huddersfield-born businessman Hanson was the multi-millionaire heir to a Yorkshire transport family and, with showbiz marriages notoriously short-lived affairs, Audrey's mother felt he was a good match for her daughter.

The stylish, successful, and sensible Audrey Hepburn was on the way up. Less than five years after landing back in Britain, her career was about to take off in a big way. When she crossed the Atlantic in 1951 to star on Broadway she had plenty of time to contemplate her bright future. Air travel was yet to become commonplace and the ocean liner on which she traveled took nearly three weeks to make the crossing.

She landed to be greeted by a scrum of reporters and a gaggle of flashbulb-popping photographers including Richard Avedon, then of *Bazaar* magazine, who captured some early iconic images of the elfin beauty. "The first thing I saw was the Statue of Liberty," she later recalled. "The second, Richard Avedon."

A Broadway triumph in *Gigi* would put Audrey firmly on the acting map. But that success was hard-won as she needed a combination of vocal coaching and old-fashioned hard work to make the grade and justify author Colette's faith in her. Impresario Gilbert Miller sacked her more than once in the weeks before curtain up, feeling she lacked the sophistication the part demanded—but realized there was no time to replace her, so both sides put their differences to one side and persevered.

The show itself was a success, Audrey's own performance garnering unanimous praise. "Fresh and frisky as a puppy out of a tub," the *New York Post* report gleefully reported, suggesting that the sophistication side of things had still to be fully mastered. Hepburn's grace of movement was down to her dancing background, and she continued dance classes while in New York. "I'm halfway between a dancer and an actress," she commented. "I've got to learn."

Certainly the fact the camera loved her made Audrey's ascension to stardom that much easier. At least, after she'd shed the stone she put on through high living during her Atlantic crossing! And while she was the epitome of womanhood, she would not, unlike most of her contemporaries, pose for risqué "cheesecake" photos. Her quote "I think sex is overrated" may have been tongue in cheek, but her innocence remained an essential part of her charm.

> ***"I think sex is overrated. I don't have sex appeal and I know it. As a matter of fact, I think I'm rather funny looking. My teeth are funny, for one thing, and I have none of the attributes usually required for a movie queen, including the shapeliness."***
> **Audrey Hepburn**

The curtain rose on *Gigi* in November 1951 at the Fulton Theatre and only fell at the end of May 1952 due to its star's movie commitments. Apparently on seeing her name in lights for the first time, Hepburn reportedly said, "Oh, dear. And I've still got to learn how to act!"

ABOVE: Audrey wears a billowing net dress with ostrich plume during a preview held by fashion designers Honoria Plesch and David De Bethell at the Palace Theatre London. The preview featured gowns and hats for *Sauce Piquante,* April 17, 1950. *Mirrorpix*

RIGHT: Audrey with the cast of a Christmas Party revue at the Cambridge Theatre, December 9, 1949. *Keystone/Getty Images*

ABOVE: Audrey Hepburn in January 1951. *Mirrorpix*

LEFT: Another Christmas Party, this one in 1950 for *Picturegoer* magazine: L–R: Derek Farr, Helen Cherry, Joan Greenwood, Richard Todd, Audrey Hepburn, and Phyllis Calvert. "God's gift to publicity men is a heart-shattering young woman," said *Picturegoer*, "with a style of her own…"
Popperfoto/Getty Images

LIFE IN ENGLAND

"My mother would have been better off in Vienna, or anywhere in Italy or France—anywhere where music and art were of equal importance to food and drink." Audrey Hepburn

Audrey was no stranger to England when she came over in 1948. Born to a British father, she had British citizenship, had been schooled at public schools in Kent and spoke English fluently. So after the war, it was to England that Audrey and her mother traveled to help her make her mark. As we have seen, she hoped to become a ballerina, but quickly realized that she was too tall to be a leading prima ballerina.

The obvious showbiz plan B was to try out on stage, and it was but a small step from chorus line to acting in films.

A struggling actress desperate to break out of anonymity, Audrey had something about her even at a young age that made her different. She made an impression on all she

LEFT: *Picture Post* was published from 1938 to 1957. The December 15, 1951, cover is of Audrey. *Bert Hardy/Picture Post/IPC Magazines/Getty Images*

met—from James Hanson who wanted to marry her to Alec Guinness, with whom she worked briefly. During rehearsals for the Rio de Janeiro airport scene in *The Lavender Hill Mob*, he could not take his eyes off her. Ian Woodward in *Audrey Hepburn: Fair Lady of the Screen* continues the story: "He [Alec Guinness] excused himself from the rehearsal for a few minutes and telephoned his agent. 'I don't know if she can act,' he said, 'but a real film star has just wafted on to the set. Someone should get her under contract before we lose her to the Americans.' "

Audrey's big break came when she was spotted by Robert Lennard, casting director of Associated British Pictures Corporation, at Ciro's nightclub where she was working on Cecil Landeau's *Summer Nights*. Lennard recommended her to director Mario Zampi and this led to a small part in the film *Laughter in Paradise*. The rest is history: she signed with Associated British, and later that company "came to a lucrative agreement by which Paramount had exclusive rights to her services" as David Shipman said in his obituary of Audrey in *The Independent*.

The photographs in this section show Audrey in England as a young actress—photo shoots and publicity shots.

ABOVE: Audrey keeping cool with two of the cast of *Sauce Tartare* on roof of the Cambridge Theatre. L–R: Aud Johannsen, Enid Smeeden and Audrey. *Ron Case/Keystone/Getty Images*

ABOVE: Audrey rehearsing at the barre. *Silver Screen Collection/Getty Images*

A young Audrey modeling a bonnet in May 1951. *Popperfoto/Getty Images*

Audrey photographed in the seaside village of Rottingdean, Sussex. *Popperfoto/Getty Images*

ABOVE: Photo shoot by the Sussex coast. *Popperfoto/Getty Images*

AUDREY AND JAMES HANSON

"Love at first sight." Audrey Hepburn

As a young man James Hanson (1922–2004), later Baron Hanson and well-known corporate raider, was something of a playboy with a penchant for actresses—he dated Jean Simmons and Joan Collins before Audrey. At 6ft 4in he made a distinctive figure when he met Audrey Hepburn at a cocktail party in Mayfair at Les Ambassadeurs. She called it "love at first sight." They met for lunch the next day and had not been dating for many months before they became engaged—he traveled to New York for *Gigi's* premiere to proffer an engagement ring. Shortly before the wedding, it was postponed. The wedding presents had been bought, the wedding dress had been ordered, and as Hanson himself said, "It was a strange situation. My mother had got the fifty chickens ready for the wedding reception and we had all the presents, but the fact was Audrey just did not want to get married at the time." After several months of postponing wedding plans, she ended her engagement with Hanson.

At a November 29, 2011, auction a collection of correspondence and papers from Miss Joan Mayall, who worked as James Hanson's private secretary for many years, was sold. It included a letter dated September 10, 1952, from James Hanson thanking Joan Mayall for a wedding gift of napkin rings; a printed official announcement card from Baroness van Heemstra of the marriage; Joan Mayall's wedding invitation; and a printed cancellation card that reads:

ABOVE: Audrey Hepburn with James Hanson. Mirrorpix

"Baroness Ella van Heemstra much regrets to announce that the wedding of her daughter Audrey Hepburn to James Hanson, arranged to take place on 30th September, 1952, at Huddersfield Parish Church, is unavoidably postponed and will take place in New York later this year."

The wedding dress had been made by the Fontana sisters—the couturiers to the stars in Italy. A simple dress of ivory silk with a large bow underneath the bust, after Audrey Hepburn called the wedding off Audrey told the Fontanas, "I want my dress to be worn by another girl for her wedding, perhaps someone who couldn't ever afford a dress like mine, the most beautiful, poor Italian girl you can find." It went to Amabile Altobella who married Adelino Solda, a farm worker … and had a long, happy marriage.

Audrey and James Hanson in Rome during 1952. *Bettmann/Corbis*

GIGI (1951)

Director: Raymond Roulear
Producer: Gilbert Miller

Audrey Hepburn – Gigi
Josephine Brown – Mme. Alvarez
Michael Evans – Gaston

Author Colette and playwright Anita Loos had been working on a stage adaptation of *Gigi* for years. Colette's 1944 novella is about a young Parisian girl, who is being groomed to become a courtesan, and Gaston, who falls in love with her and eventually marries her. The story is based, Colette said, on a conversation she overheard in 1914 between two women discussing their astonishment at a young girl winning a marriage proposal from a wealthy older man after refusing to become his mistress. Colette spotted Audrey while she was on location for *Monte Carlo Baby* and insisted on her involvement. Audrey sailed to New York on the *Queen Mary*.

The play previewed in Philadelphia on November 8, and then opened on Broadway at the Fulton Theatre, New York, on November 24, 1951, to good reviews. The show ran for 219 performances and won Audrey the 1952 Theatre World Award. It was later adapted as a film musical of the same title in 1958, with Leslie Caron in Hepburn's role.

ABOVE: Audrey as Gigi and Cathleen Nesbitt as her aunt, Alicia de St. Ephlam, on Broadway. *Bettmann/Corbis*

RIGHT: Author Anita Loos, Audrey, and director Raymond Rouleau at rehearsal, November 16, 1951. *Bettmann/Corbis*

THE SECRET PEOPLE (1952)

Director: Thorold Dickinson
Ealing Studios
Released August 1952. Black and white

Valentina Cortese – Maria Brentano
Serge Reggiani – Louis Balan
Charles Goldner – Anselmo
Audrey Hepburn – Nora Brentano
Angela Fouldes – Nora Brentano as a child
Megs Jenkins – Penny

"LOOK OUT FOR THIS MAN! HE LIVES! AND LOVES! AND MURDERS!" **Tagline**

The Secret People was one of young Audrey's earliest starring roles. While she would appear in bigger budget productions like 1951's *Lavender Hill Mob*, her screen time barely topped the ten-second mark.

The film was a thriller by revered British writer and director Thorold Dickinson. It was one of his last before he moved from making films to educating others about them as a university professor.

Audrey starred alongside Italian Valentina Cortese as Nora and Maria Brentano respectively, sisters whose father was murdered. They are caught up in an assassination plan in Paris where an innocent bystander is killed by a misplaced bomb.

The confusing plotline is almost forgotten with Audrey's performance. In a role similar to her own life she plays a World War II survivor with a passion for ballet. She dazzled the audience with extended dance scenes that would show her detractors she could have made it.

Despite its promise, the film failed at the box-office and fell into obscurity as Hepburn's career soared. Now considered a minor cult classic, it is a great opportunity to view Audrey during her early career in a part that lasts longer than a few seconds.

LEFT: Audrey and Serge Reggiani on the set. *Popperfoto/Getty Images*

RIGHT: All that ballet training paid off! *Popperfoto/Getty Images*

3 OSCAR WINNER 1952–60

"I act the same way now as I did forty years ago … with feeling instead of technique. All my life I've been in situations where I've had no technique, but if you feel enough you can get away with murder."
Audrey Hepburn

Britain would remember 1953 as the year Queen Elizabeth II was crowned in Westminster Abbey, and Edmund Hillary was first to scale the summit of Mount Everest. But in cinematic terms the event of the year took place in August when William Wyler's *Roman Holiday* premiered in New York. And it was a Brit, Audrey Hepburn, who was the centre of attention. She had signed up for the role even before *Gigi*, and the Big Apple was familiar territory by now after her Broadway triumph. But this big-screen appearance would flash the image of this "child-woman with flaring nostrils and upswept brows" across the known world to every corner, captivating all with "a smile both wistful and radiant," not to mention those "dark, expressive eyes." It was her seventh film, but the first she had carried on her slim shoulders.

This quantum leap in performance would be recognized at March 1954's Academy Awards. While proceedings were dominated by *From Here To Eternity*, which equaled the record set by *Gone With The Wind* in winning eight Oscars, Audrey's was the name on the Best Actress statuette. Minutes after accepting the award at the Center Theater in New York, she realized that she'd left it in the ladies' room. Without turning an elegant hair,

she retraced her steps to retrieve the award and pose for photographs.

She received another Academy Award nomination for her next movie *Sabrina*, like *Roman Holiday* a romantic comedy. Hepburn was "terrified" of co-star Humphrey Bogart, but got on rather better with the younger William Holden; the male pair played brothers with whom Audrey, a modern-day Cinderella, had fallen in love and could not choose between.

The end of her romance with James Hanson was hastened by the near-impossible work schedules both faced. The pair had become engaged in the most romantic of circumstances when James flew the Atlantic to be at the *Gigi* premiere. His work saw him commuting constantly between America, Canada, and Britain, and he and Audrey had been able to spend time together during *Gigi*'s Broadway run.

The wedding had been planned to take place between the end of the play and the start of shooting of the film that spring. The Fontana sisters designed an ivory satin wedding gown, but the nuptials were postponed at the last minute when Audrey was obliged to fly straight to Rome immediately after closing night.

Returning to fulfil her US touring obligations with

Audrey shows off her Oscar. *Getty Images*

ABOVE: Audrey Hepburn, 1952. *Popperfoto/Getty Images*

RIGHT: Ed Sullivan celebrates the fourth anniversary of his TV show "Toast of the Town," June 3, 1952. L–R, front row, Rex Harrison, Audrey, Ed Sullivan, Ginny Simms, and Jack Smith; back row, John Wray, Marlo Lewis, Ray Bloch, and the "Toastettes" look on. *Bettmann/Corbis*

Gigi, Hepburn announced the end of the engagement halfway through the eight-month tour. Having worked so hard to establish herself, it was perhaps the logical decision to let head rule heart, but the split was an amicable one.

Audrey was not to remain alone for long. Having returned to London in July 1953 to attend the British premiere of *Roman Holiday* she met American actor/director Mel Ferrer at a social gathering. He had been invited by a friend, *Roman Holiday* leading man Gregory Peck. Twelve years Audrey's senior, Ferrer had been married three times, twice to his first wife Frances, and it was predictable that Audrey's mother Ella heard alarm bells ringing. (As it happened, their relationship would survive until 1967.) Mel said of Audrey, "My first impression of Audrey when we finally saw each other was how simple and direct she was. She was gentle, delicate and sensitive. But full of life and sparkle."

The tall, darkly handsome Ferrer had been tipped as the next Orson Welles and he clearly had plans for Audrey. He sent her the script for a French play, *Ondine,* which was set to be staged on Broadway. She loved it, figuring it was the right time for a "serious dramatic part" that contrasted with her earlier work, and agreed to take the role on the understanding that Mel would be her co-star.

The production made great use of her nimbleness and dancer's suppleness, and she shone as the water nymph who could only gain a soul by marrying a male human. While a Tony Award was hers for the taking, *Ondine* never made it to the big screen—and, due to Audrey's burgeoning fame and price tag, it would be her last stage production.

Newsweek magazine reported that queues for the box office went round the block, reflecting not only *Ondine*'s virtues but the big-screen success of the just-

released *Roman Holiday*. This multi-media domination was, however, very much the product of hard work, Hepburn herself saying that she put "a tremendous amount of effort into every little morsel that comes out." She was still learning her trade, and was humble enough to admit it rather than let fame go to her head.

But fame exacts a price—and, like it or not, Audrey Hepburn was now very much a media darling. The long lenses of the press would be a constant companion until the end of her life. It was scarcely a year since her Stateside-bound ocean liner had docked, and half a dozen since her showbusiness voyage had began, but here she was rivaling the likes of Marilyn Monroe for newsworthiness. But the physical and mental stresses of the past months were quickly catching up with the slightly built actress.

The Academy Award for *Roman Holiday*—so unexpected she didn't have any champagne on ice—and Tony for *Ondine* had been bestowed a matter of days apart, and public expectation was now immense. While Audrey said all the sensible things—"I can't allow this award or all the public acclaim to turn my head," she insisted at the Oscars—the strain was now showing. She was advised to quit *Ondine* just three months into its run, suffering from exhaustion, but her retreat to an Alpine resort in Switzerland saw her chased and virtually imprisoned by the world's media.

A concerned Mel Ferrer flew to Switzerland and took an engagement ring in his luggage. His proposal was accepted, despite his future mother in law's doubts, and Audrey became the third Mrs. Ferrer in a civil ceremony on September 24 at Buoche on the shores of Lake Lucerne. The next day they repeated their vows at a religious ceremony in a chapel below the mountain.

A four-day honeymoon sealed Audrey's love affair not just with Mel but with Switzerland, the country she would call home from then on. (The clear air was

ABOVE and LEFT: Film actress Audrey Hepburn in London on her return from shooting *Roman Holiday* on May 21, 1953. *Mirrorpix*

the ideal antidote to the asthma to which she had sometimes been prone.) A week together near Cinecitta in Italy, where Mel was filming *La Madre*—they were pursued though country lanes by carloads of press photographers—was followed by a return to Bürgenstock where they learned that Audrey was expecting. Sadly she would lose the child in the following spring, the first of a number of miscarriages she would suffer in her life.

November 1954 saw Audrey return to Holland for the first time since the war. She accepted an invitation from the League of Dutch Military War Invalids to carry out a five-day fund-raising tour, an early example of her philanthropic nature. "As you get older," she said, "you remember you have another hand: the first is to help yourself, the second is to help others."

In contrast to her *Roman Holiday* triumph, Audrey unusually found herself in a critically savaged movie when in 1956 she starred as Natasha Rostov in *War And Peace*. The $6 million feature, shot in Italy, was overblown, and the screenplay required no fewer than

ABOVE: The great photographer Richard Avedon said of Audrey, "She has achieved in herself her ultimate portrait." Here he has a front row seat at a show in Paris, in February 1958. *Hulton-Deutsch Collection/Corbis*

RIGHT: *Sabrina* (1954) saw Audrey wearing a divine Givenchy flower-patterned dress. *Underwood & Underwood/Corbis*

ABOVE: Audrey receives an Oscar for Best Actress at the Center Theater in New York on March 25, 1954. *Bettmann/Corbis*

LEFT: Audrey in 1954. *Bettmann/Corbis*

six writers to complete. But her performance was singled out as the exception. One consolation was the presence of husband Mel as Prince Andrei, though his performance didn't escape criticism. (Audrey's fee for the movie was three and a half times Mel's $100,000 salary.)

Hepburn recalled the shooting as physically demanding, not least wearing "velvets and furs in August," and rated it her hardest acting challenge of her career. It proved demanding of audiences too, and at

three and a half hours it possessed what one critic called "length without depth." The critics' wrath was turned on Henry Fonda, who was an unconvincing Count Pierre Bezukhov, but Audrey escaped unscathed.

Next up was her first screen musical, *Funny Face*, again set in Europe but a movie with a remarkably light touch. Her wardrobe, designed by Givenchy, made as many headlines as she did (the designer would be contracted to supply her wardrobe from then on), and

the rapport she struck up with 57-year-old veteran Fred Astaire was plain for all to see. In common with her marriage, she was regularly cast opposite leading men who were considerably older than herself.

Audrey had turned down the title role in the movie version of her stage triumph *Gigi* (eventually screened in 1958 with Leslie Caron in the title role) to make *Funny Face*, going against her agent's views after reading the script. Interestingly the plot—a photographer "discovers"

ABOVE: Actress Faye Emerson congratulates Tony winners David Wayne (*Teahouse of the August Moon*) and Audrey. The presentation was made at the 8th Annual Antoinette Perry Awards at the Plaza Hotel in New York City three nights after Audrey won the Oscar. *Bettmann/Corbis*

LEFT: Audrey changing after coming from the 46th Street Theater before she received her Oscar. *Bettmann/Corbis*

a model and grooms her for stardom in *My Fair Lady* fashion—was based on the life of high-society snapper Richard Avedon, who not so long ago had snapped her on arrival in New York City.

"There is not a woman alive who does not dream of looking like Audrey Hepburn."
Hubert de Givenchy

Audrey was hot box-office property, so was able to stipulate a $150,000 fee plus a suite at a Paris hotel for herself and Mel and, as ever, a Givenchy wardrobe. The month spent filming the film's Paris scenes was timed to coincide with Mel's shooting of *Paris Does Strange Things*.

As well as dancing, with which she was well acquainted, Audrey was asked to sing several songs in the film, which she considered a particular challenge. Four weeks of rehearsal and coaching preceded her efforts, which paralleled Astaire's difficult transition from dancer to actor/singer (his first screen test infamously read: "Can't act. Can't sing. Balding. Can dance a little").

Audrey downplayed her all-round abilities, but was honest about having to meet new challenges. "I was asked to act when I couldn't act. I was asked to sing 'Funny Face' when I couldn't sing and dance with Fred Astaire when I couldn't dance—do all kinds of things I wasn't prepared for. Then I tried like mad to cope with it." In the end, critics described *Funny Face* as a glossy fashion show, with the emphasis on her looks and wardrobe. She also said about filming *Funny Face* while

LEFT: Audrey and Mel in *Cerebral Palsy*, a Benefit Performance of Ringling Brothers and Barnum Bailey Circus, March 31, 1954. *Bettmann/Corbis*

RIGHT: Portrait of Audrey Hepburn, June 1954. Immortalized with a star on the Walk of Fame, Audrey is one of Hollywood's icons, consistently voted one of its greatest stars. *Bettmann/Corbis*

coping with extreme Paris weather and a grumpy co-star: "Here I've been waiting for 20 years to dance with Fred Astaire, and what do I get? Mud in my eye!"

> *"She was so gracious and graceful that everybody fell in love with her after five minutes. Everybody was in love with this girl, I included. My problem was that I am a guy who speaks in his sleep. I toss around and talk and talk … But fortunately, my wife's first name is Audrey as well."*
> **Billy Wilder**

Next came *Love In The Afternoon*, another Billy Wilder-directed project which saw her cast opposite the near three decades older Gary Cooper. It was a total mismatch that blighted the result. Audrey seemed to want to distance herself from the project as it continued, and during the shoot in Paris had made weekend trips to the south of France where Mel had been filming *The Vintage*. On its completion she left Europe to spend Christmas at a desert resort near Palm Springs, with her husband and his children, Pepa and Mark. "He is a protective husband and I like it," was her response to enquiries about their relationship. "Most women do …"

> *"She was always on time and ready to work. She knew her lines, in fact, her suggestions elevated the lines — she could give lessons on celebrity behavior."*
> **Janis Blackschleger**

Audrey was constantly in demand, and was offered many more roles than she could possibly have fitted into her schedule. She turned down most of them, including the lead role in 1959's *The Diary of Anne Frank* because she then felt it would bring back too many painful wartime memories. (She would, however, narrate a musical adaptation in 1990.) Of *The Diary of Anne Frank*, she said "I was given the book in Dutch, in galley form, in 1946 by a friend. I read it … and it destroyed me. It does this to many people when they first read it but I was not reading it as a book, as printed pages. This was my life. I didn't know what I was going to read. I've never been the same again, it affected me so deeply."

She was happy at this stage to let her husband take the lead in career terms, but Mel Ferrer's track record as either actor or director was, unsurprisingly, nowhere near as impressive as hers. The 1957 made for TV movie *Mayerling*, about the love life of the crown prince of Austria, was rated as "pallid" by *The New York Times*, and the following year's *Green Mansions* would be the last project the two would work on together.

1959 movie *The Nun's Story* was to prove a physical hurdle too far for the still physically insubstantial Hepburn. Location work took place in the Belgian Congo and Audrey's dehydration there led to a bad case of kidney stones when she returned to Italy to finish filming. While *The Nun's Story*, telling of the moral dilemmas faced by real-life Sister Luke in Africa during World War II, made more money at the box office than any Warner Brothers film to date, it failed to win one of the eight Oscars it was nominated for, including Audrey for Best Actress. It was, however, a foretaste of her humanitarian work in Africa some three decades later.

The physical problems involved in completing film roles reared their head again, quite literally, in 1959 when, while shooting *The Unforgiven* in Mexico, Audrey was thrown from a horse. She broke her back and had to complete filming a month later with the aid of an orthopedic brace, all the while fretting about the health of the child she was carrying.

Shortly after *The Unforgiven* was completed, Audrey miscarried for the second time. Husband Mel revealed

Married in 1954, Audrey miscarried in March 1955 but signed up for *War and Peace* which filmed July–October. This photograph was taken after shooting ended, October 28, 1955. *Michael Ochs Archives/Getty Images*

that the tragic event "has broken her heart and mine." She entered a deep depression, lost weight and smoked heavily. But happily, less than six months later, she found she was pregnant again. Putting family before profession, she turned down all work including a role in *West Side Story,* until the baby was born. The only work commitment she made was to star in *Breakfast At Tiffany's,* but shooting was to commence only after the birth.

The 1950s had been an incredible decade. She had advanced at rapid pace from being an unknown waif-like dancer to an acclaimed stage and screen actress whose fame and fortune was unparalleled. Yet she seemed to have managed it while keeping both feet firmly on the ground. "I probably hold the distinction of being one movie star who, by all laws of logic, should never have made it," she said. "At each stage of my career, I lacked the experience."

The 1950s had been a rollercoaster experience that neither she nor her worldwide army of fans would ever forget. Could the forthcoming decade be anywhere near as exciting?

LEFT: Audrey burst onto the Hollywood scene when she was very young and her sensational beauty and elegance captivated stars, moguls, and viewing public alike. *Archive Photos/Getty Images*

BELOW: Audrey and her mother in the grounds of the Château de Vitry, west of Paris, where Audrey was doing location work for *Love In The Afternoon. Bettmann/Corbis*

THIS PAGE and RIGHT: Audrey in a November 3, 1954, photo shoot. *Mirrorpix*

ABOVE: Audrey Hepburn and Jack Hawkins in 1955. *Mirrorpix*

RIGHT: November 8, 1955, image was taken by John Springer who took the classic *Breakfast at Tiffany's* shot. *John Springer Collection/Corbis*

AUDREY & MEL FERRER
1954-68

"If I get married, I want to be very married."
Audrey Hepburn

Audrey would have married James Hanson but felt that their different schedules would keep them apart. Mel Ferrer, however, was in the same business as she. They met in July 1953 at a party hosted by mutual friend Gregory Peck. Audrey's co-star in *Roman Holiday*, Peck and Mel had set up a summer playhouse in Peck's hometown of La Jolla, an affluent beach community just north of San Diego. Audrey knew all about La Jolla and had seen Mel in *Lili*. Audrey was fascinated by Mel and told him she'd love to do a play with him on Broadway if he could come up with the right project. Mel was also fascinated, and immediately went home to the United States where he set in train divorce proceedings with his estranged wife. Next he trawled through plays to find a suitable vehicle for Audrey and himself. He chose *Ondine*—a brilliant choice that would get Audrey a Tony award. He showed her the script in late 1953 while she was shooting *Sabrina* and she accepted. The play opened on February 18, 1954, and seven months later, on September 24, Audrey and Mel were married. The next day they were married publicly in a chapel in Bürgenstock. Two of Mel's children—Pepa and Mark—were there along with his sister Terry and Audrey's mother. The groom wore a navy suit with white tie; the bride a white organdy Givenchy dress.

Mel and Audrey were married for fourteen years, during which time he managed her career and saw her become one of the highest-paid stars in Hollywood. Some said he tried to control her; certainly, her mother didn't get on with him. They tried hard for children. Audrey had two miscarriages before their son, Sean. In the end, the marriage finished in divorce in 1968 amid rumors of infidelity on both sides.

LEFT: Audrey and Mel leave the chapel after their wedding at Bürgenstock. The flower girl and page are the children of hotel owner Fritz Frey, whose resort has been the actress's retreat for about ten weeks, September 25, 1954. Audrey wears a dress designed by Balmain. *Getty Images*

BELOW: Audrey and Mel arrive in London December 30, 1954. *Mirrorpix*

73

ABOVE: Mel, Audrey, and Mr. Famous arrive at Zurich airport, May 1959. *Keystone/Corbis*
RIGHT: Photoshoot in Bürgenstock, May 1959. *STR/Keystone/Corbis*

ROMAN HOLIDAY (1953)

Director: William Wyler
Paramount Pictures
Released September 1953. Black and white

Gregory Peck – Joe Bradley
Audrey Hepburn – Princess Ann
Eddie Albert – Irving Radovich
Hartley Power – Mr. Hennessy
Harcourt Williams – Ambassador
Margaret Rawlings – Countess Vereberg

"Thanks to their first glimpse of Audrey Hepburn in Roman Holiday, half a generation of young females stopped stuffing their bras and teetering on stiletto heels."
The New York Times

Roman Holiday announced Hepburn's arrival as a major player in Hollywood. Directed and produced by Academy award winner William Wyler, the romantic comedy would see her snare an Oscar.

Hepburn stars opposite Gregory Peck as Ann, a princess in Rome who finds herself in the company of journalist Joe Bradley, played by Peck. Despite his bet with his editor to grab a scoop on the princess, Peck's character finds himself falling in love with her. Audrey sparkled in the role of a royal who just wanted to experience a normal life. The classic love story had a heartbreaking end, however, as Princess Ann returns to her royal life despite her love for Bradley, signaling that their love can never flourish.

After earning the role through a screen test, an until-then largely unknown Hepburn captured the attention of her audience and critics alike, bursting onto the scene and winning a Best Actress hat-trick of a Golden Globe, a BAFTA, and an Oscar.

Audrey Hepburn had emerged in quite some style, and it would be the first classic film in a career that would enchant millions.

LEFT: Audrey was never more captivating than in *Roman Holiday* filmed June–October 1952. Rome made a breathtaking backdrop. *Bettmann/Corbis*

RIGHT: A special benefit premiere of *Roman Holiday* was held at the Village Theater in Westwood on September 14, 1953, with the proceeds going to the expansion fund of the Santa Monica Hospital. *Michael Ochs Archives/Getty Images*

ONDINE (1954)

Director: Alfred Lunt
Produced by the Playwrights' Company by
arrangement with Schuyler Watts

Mel Ferrer – Hans Ritter
Audrey Hepburn – Ondine
John Alexander – Auguste
Peter Brandon – Bertram

Audrey had told Mel Ferrer she'd love to do a play with him on Broadway if he could come up with the right project. Jean Giraudoux wrote *Ondine* in 1939. A play based on an ancient legend about a water nymph's doomed love for a medieval knight, Ferrer showed the script to Audrey who accepted the role (and so saved him from financial embarrassment). Once Audrey had said yes, preparations for the play began in earnest … and so did a deep romance that would lead to their marriage. After previews in Boston *Ondine* opened at the 46th Street Theater on Broadway and ran for 157 sold-out performances from February 18 through July 3, 1954. The intense interest in the play was fueled as much by fascination in the two stars as for its excellent dialog and Tony-winning sets and costumes. Audrey's revealing net bodysuit helped as well!

In March Audrey received the Tony for best on stage actress for her interpretation of *Ondine* … three days after she picked up an Oscar for *Roman Holiday*. Mel was at her side on both occasions. In the end, her physical frailty led to the play coming to an end early and Audrey went to Switzerland to recuperate. While there, Mel would join her and propose marriage.

"She has authentic charm. Most people simply have nice manners."
Alfred Lunt (Director)

LEFT and RIGHT: Mel and Audrey in *Ondine*, February 21, 1954. *Bettmann/ Corbis.*

SABRINA (1954)

Director: Billy Wilder
Paramount Pictures
Released October 1954. Black and
white

Humphrey Bogart – Linus Larrabee
Audrey Hepburn – Sabrina Fairchild
William Holden – David Larrabee
Walter Hampden – Oliver Larrabee
John Williams – Thomas Fairchild
Martha Hyer – Elizabeth Tyson

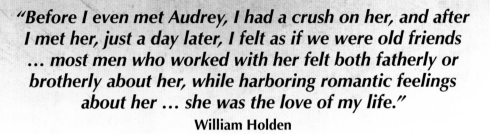

"Before I even met Audrey, I had a crush on her, and after I met her, just a day later, I felt as if we were old friends … most men who worked with her felt both fatherly or brotherly about her, while harboring romantic feelings about her … she was the love of my life."
William Holden

Audrey rode the wave of *Roman Holiday*'s success with another romantic comedy in 1954. *Sabrina* went on to be almost as successful, with an Oscar and four nominations.

The cast was strong and reflected Hepburn's rapidly rising stock as she starred alongside previous Academy Award winners in William Holden and Humphrey Bogart. The two leading men played David and Linus Larrabee respectively, immensely rich brothers with affections for chauffeur's daughter Sabrina (Hepburn).

The film follows Sabrina's desire to be noticed by David, who falls for her after her return from Paris. Linus fears David's lucrative marriage to a fellow aristocrat is in jeopardy and sets about deterring Sabrina, but ultimately falls for her as well. Of the role Audrey said, "Sabrina was a dreamer who lived a fairy-tale, and she was a romantic, an incorrigible romantic, which I am. I could never be cynical. I wouldn't dare. I'd roll over and die before that."

Hepburn and Bogart end the film together and it was a hit, with Audrey narrowly missing out on a second Best Actress Oscar to Grace Kelly for her role in *The Country Girl*.

The Billy Wilder-directed movie was the subject of a remake in 1995 starring Julia Ormond, Harrison Ford and Greg Kinnear, though needless to say it failed to rival Hepburn's original in any respect.

LEFT: Audrey and William Holden became romantically involved during the filming of *Sabrina*: she only broke off the relationship when she discovered that he had had a vasectomy because she was desperate to have children. *Bettmann/Corbis*

RIGHT: Publicity still for *Sabrina. Bettmann/Corbis*

WAR AND PEACE (1956)

Director: King Vidor
Paramount Pictures
Released August 1956. Technicolor

Audrey Hepburn – Natasha Rostova
Henry Fonda – Pierre Bezukhov
Mel Ferrer – Prince Andrei Bolkonsky
Vittorio Gassman – Anatol Kuragin
Herbert Lom – Napoleon
Oskar Homolka – Field Marshal Kutuzov
Anita Ekberg – Helene Kuragina

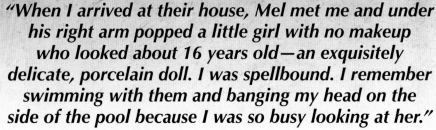

"When I arrived at their house, Mel met me and under his right arm popped a little girl with no makeup who looked about 16 years old — an exquisitely delicate, porcelain doll. I was spellbound. I remember swimming with them and banging my head on the side of the pool because I was so busy looking at her."
Jeremy Brett (who played Audrey's brother
Ensign Count Nicholas Rostov)

The adaptation of Leo Tolstoy's renowned novel was another high point in Hepburn's blossoming film career. This movie was nearly as epic as its literary version, with a running time of nearly three and a half hours.

Hepburn was a sought-after leading lady at this point, as the cast and estimated budget of $6 million indicated.

It was one of the last films made by director King Vidor in a career that began as long ago as 1913. Audrey portrayed Natasha Rostova opposite two leading men, Henry Fonda as Count Pierre Bezukhov and real-life husband Mel Ferrer as Prince Andrei Bolkonsky.

The subject-matter did not have a negative effect at the box office, nor did the mix of English and Italian dialogue; the nineteenth-century tale of the French invasion of Russia proved a success with audiences, with Hepburn being nominated for Best Actress at the 1957 Golden Globes, and Best British Actress at the BAFTAs.

Audrey Hepburn was proving her talent in different genres. Fans and critics alike were hailing her as the awards and nominations continued to flood in.

FAR LEFT: Audrey and Henry Fonda. *Bettmann/Corbis*

LEFT: Audrey at the Plaza for the premiere of *War and Peace* November 18, 1956. *Mirrorpix*

FUNNY FACE (1957)

Director: Stanley Donen
Paramount Pictures
Released February 1957. Technicolor

Gregory Peck – Joe Bradley
Audrey Hepburn – Jo Stockton
Fred Astaire – Dick Avery
Kay Thompson – Maggie Prescott
Michel Auclair – Prof. Emile Flostre
Robert Flemyng – Paul Duval
Dovima – Marion

"People don't realize how educated she was. She spoke several languages fluently. She had a wonderful speaking voice—extremely cultured, with wonderful pronunciation. She was a joy to listen to. She never raised her voice, so you were drawn in, you had to listen carefully, and you wanted to." **Stanley Donen** (director, *Funny Face, Charade, Two for the Road*)

This movie musical film shares only its name with the Broadway production of three decades earlier; while it used some of the songs, the plot was completely different. Another thing the musicals shared was leading man Fred Astaire, who would star alongside Hepburn for the first time.

Audrey plays an intelligent bookshop owner named Jo Stockton who comes into contact with fashion magazine editor Maggie Prescott (Kay Thompson) and Astaire's character, photographer Dick Avery, when they arrive at the bookshop in search of fashion's next big thing.

Lured by a trip to Paris to see her idol Emile Flostre, Stockton eventually agrees to model for Avery, inevitably falling in love with him.

Funny Face was directed by *Singin' In The Rain* co-director Stanley Donen and, with some songs by famed composers George and Ira Gershwin, was considered a heavyweight musical.

It was certainly a departure from the great literature of *War And Peace*, but Hepburn once again demonstrated her diversity. The plot while simple, wooed audiences, though it missed out on an Academy Award despite four nominations.

FAR LEFT: Another wonderful costume for Audrey. *Paramount/Getty Images*

LEFT: Audrey and Fred Astaire on set. *Sunset Boulevard/Corbis*

LOVE IN THE AFTERNOON (1957)

Director: Billy Wilder
Allied Artists Pictures
Released June 1957. Black and white

Gary Cooper – Frank Flannagan
Audrey Hepburn – Ariane Chavasse
Maurice Chevalier – Claude Chavasse
John McGiver – Monsieur X
Van Doude – Michel
Lise Bourdin – Madame X

"Audrey was known for something which has disappeared, and that is elegance, grace and manners."
Billy Wilder

Audrey was reunited with director Billy Wilder for this romantic comedy. The film had literary merit, being based on the novel *Ariane, Jeune Fille Russe* by French tennis player Jean Schopfer under the pseudonym of Claude Anet.

Hepburn's screen association with France continued as she played Ariane, the daughter of detective Claude Chavasse. Her task was to shadow American playboy Frank Flannagan (Gary Cooper) at the request of jealous husbands whose wives the cad was wooing.

On discovering one of the husbands plans to kill Flannagan, Ariane decides to warn him, posing as a young bachelorette. Needless to say the pair fall in love.

The fluffy "rom-com" was generally well-received, but the decision to cast 55-year-old Cooper opposite a young and beautiful Hepburn was criticized. Cary Grant was initially approached by Wilder for the role, but declined.

Hepburn was continuing to receive glowing reviews from her critics, and as the Sixties approached would be confident enough to take on more daring and diverse roles that would help cement her place as one of the all-time greats.

LEFT: For Maurice Chevalier, who made his first appearance on the Paris stage in 1904, *Love In The Afternoon* was his 30th motion picture. *Bettmann/Corbis*

RIGHT: Gary Cooper and Audrey on the set of *Love in the Afternoon*. *Cat's Collection/Corbis*

MAYERLING (1957)

Directors: Kirk Browning, Anatole Litvak
Producer's Showcase TV
Released February 4, 1957. Black and white

Mel Ferrer – Crown Prince Rudolph
Audrey Hepburn – Marie Vetsera
Lorne Greene – David Larrabee
Diana Wynyard – The Empress
Basil Sydney – Emperor
Raymond Massey – The Prime Minister

The story of Mayerling dates back to the last years of the nineteenth century and the Central European Austro-Hungarian Empire. The heir to empire, Crown Prince Rudolf of Austria—only son of Emperor Franz Josef I and Empress Elisabeth—and his mistress, Baroness Mary Vetsera, died in mysterious circumstances at a hunting lodge near the village of Mayerling southwest of Vienna, Austria. Was it a murder-suicide pact or something more sinister? All that is known is that the bodies of the archduke and the 17-year-old Baroness were discovered at Mayerling on January 30, 1889.

Anatole Litvak, a friend of the Ferrers, had previously directed a 1936 French film version of Mayerling. Audrey and Mal had agreed to play the unfortunate lovers in an episode of the American television series Producers' Showcase made for NBC. An expensive, extravagant production, with a cast of over a hundred, it was broadcast on February 24, 1957, and released as a film in Europe. It was not well received by critics: "Audrey Hepburn was called on to do little more than look beautiful and look smitten with maidenly adoration, an assignment which gave her no trouble at all," said Jay Nelson Tuck in the *New York Post*.

"Sharing the honors with Litvak was Miss Hepburn, for her vibrant and controlled love scenes and her unsophisticated youth captured the charm and compassion of this Viennese idyll. What could have been sentimental and maudlin was brought to life as a warm and feeling story. She was exquisite in her childlike beauty. Ferrer was the embodiment of soulful tragedy and if hardly the equal of Miss Hepburn in histrionics, this rates as one of his best performances to date." Variety

LEFT: Makeup artist and hairstylists prepare Audrey for a scene. *Underwood & Underwood/Corbis*

GREEN MANSIONS (1959)

Director: Mel Ferrer
Metro-Goldwyn-Mayer
Released May 1959. Panavision

Anthony Perkins – Abel
Audrey Hepburn – Rima
Lee J Cobb – Nuflo
Sessue Hayakawa – Runi
Henry Silva – Kua-ko
Nehemiah Persoff – Don Panta
Michael Pate – Priest
Estelle Hemsley – Cla Cla

"W.H. Hudson's unforgettable story of love and adventure in the South American jungles!" Tagline

Green Mansions by William Henry Hudson was supposed to be the first of a number of vehicles for Audrey and Mel, and was carefully chosen. Set in the jungle of South America, it was it was the first major film to be filmed in Panavision, had a realistic backdrop of jungle footage specially shot on location, and a performance by Audrey about which *The New York Times* critic Bosley Crowther said: "without the ethereal Miss Hepburn vaporing lightly through the Venezuelan woods, floating out to charm a masculine intruder or poise wistfully with great tears in her eyes when she makes a sad discovery of man's deceptions, this could be a pretty foolish film." In fact, Audrey was miscast—in the novel the "bird-woman" Rima was shorter, much younger, and wilder—and the box office results were dreadful.

LEFT: Audrey and Anthony Perkins star in a film directed by her husband. *Sunset Boulevard/Corbis*

THE NUN'S STORY (1959)

"In the role of the nun, Miss Hepburn is fluent and luminous. From her eyes and her eloquent expressions emerge a character that is warm and involved."

Bosley Crowther (critic *The New York Times*)

In a departure from her previous film roles Hepburn became Gabrielle van der Mal, daughter of a wealthy Belgian doctor, who leaves her life behind to become a nun.

Sister Luke as she is now known, still harbors dreams of practicing medicine herself and begins to question her decision to join the monastery. When World War II breaks out her doubts grow as she finds it difficult to stay impartial in the face of Hitler's atrocities.

This poignant drama drew many plaudits for Hepburn, who waxed lyrical about her performance in a more serious role. It was directed by Fred Zinnemann, who had been responsible for the 1953 Oscar-winning smash *From Here To Eternity*.

The film was considered a huge success and was nominated for eight Academy Awards, including one for Hepburn as Best Actress. Amazingly, it was not successful in any category.

Despite this, Hepburn gained a lot of respect as an actress who could excel in any genre, a verdict supported by her second BAFTA for best actress. She would now be remembered as much more than just "flavor of the month."

Director: Fred Zinnemann
Warner Brothers Pictures
Released July 1959. Technicolor

Audrey Hepburn – Sister Luke
Peter Finch – Dr. Fortunati
Edith Evans – Rev. Mother Emmanuel
Peggy Ashcroft – Mother Mathilde
Dean Jagger – D. Van der Mal
Mildred Dunnock – Sister Margharita
Beatrice Straight – Mother Christophe

LEFT: Audrey as Sister Luke, January 13, 1958. *Popperfoto/Getty Images*

RIGHT: Peter Finch and Audrey on set, March 22, 1958. *Bettmann/Corbis*

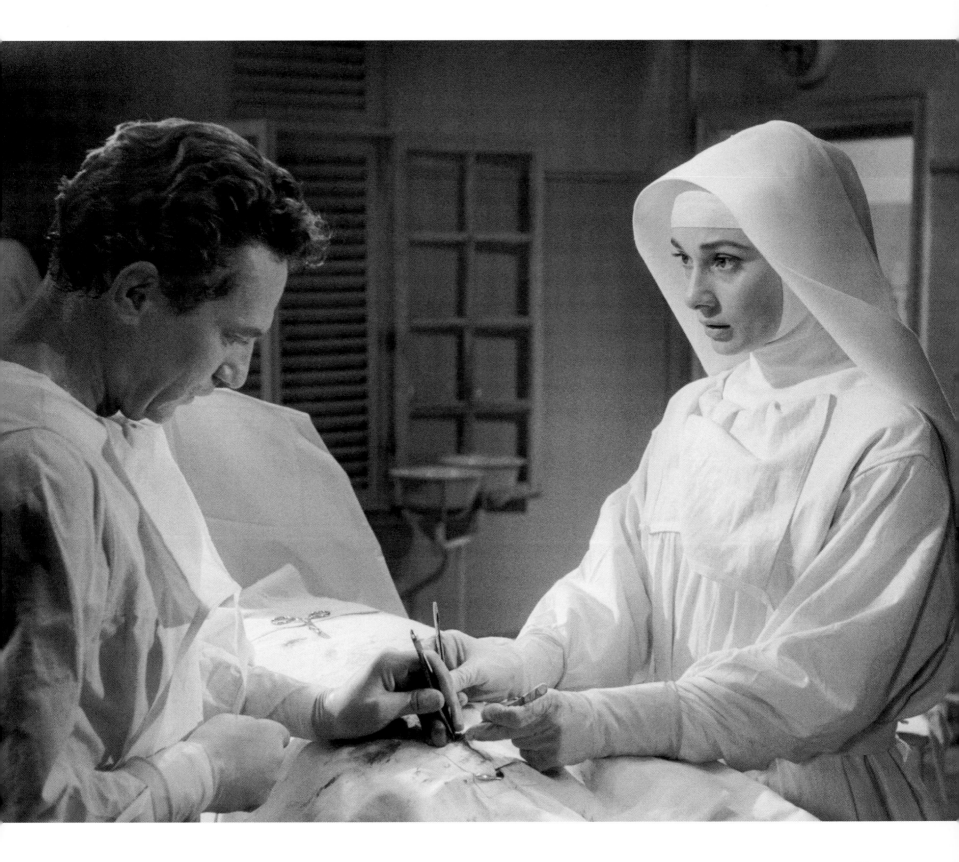

AUDREY AND GIVENCHY

"Balenciaga once said the secret of elegance is elimination. I believe that. That's why I love Hubert Givenchy ... They're clothes without ornament, with everything stripped away." Audrey Hepburn

Hubert de Givenchy was born in 1927 and started commercial fashion design after the war, working alongside the then unknown Pierre Balmain and Christian Dior for Lucien Lelong before spending four years with Elsa Schiaparelli. In 1952 he opened up his own house and first met Audrey Hepburn in 1953. The story is well known: during the shooting of *Sabrina* Audrey flew to Paris for an appointment with him. He was expecting Katharine Hepburn. He said she should choose anything she liked from his current collection, and thus a lifelong relationship was born. *Sabrina* won one Oscar—for costume design—much of the reason being Audrey's Givenchy outfits. However, in a story that could only happen in Hollywood, the Oscar went to Edith Head who had refused to let Givenchy's name appear alongside hers in the credits. Audrey Hepburn called him in Paris to apologize.

"I was very touched, but told her not to worry, because Sabrina had brought me more new clients than I could handle," Givenchy said. "But Audrey was still upset, and she made a promise to me that in the future she would make sure that it never happened again. And she kept her promise. This was one of the most marvelous things about her. She thought constantly of others." Perhaps this was also the reason that Audrey refused payment from Givenchy for using her name when the first celebrity perfume—Givenchy's *L'Interdit*—went on the market and she helped with the advertising and publicity.

The sales hook for *L'Interdit* was that it had been created by Givenchy in 1957 for Audrey's personal use, and the advertising included a Richard Avedon photograph of Audrey with the tagline, "Once she was the only woman in the world allowed to wear this perfume. *L'Interdit*. Created by Givenchy for Audrey Hepburn."

After *Sabrina*, the high point of the Hepburn-Givenchy partnership must be the iconic evening gown of black Italian satin she wore as Holly Golightly in *Breakfast At Tiffany's*. Sold by Christie's in 2006 for £467,200 ($923,187) the sleeveless, floor-length gown had a fitted bodice embellished at the back with distinctive cut-out décolleté. The skirt was slightly gathered at the waist and slit to the thigh on one side.

Theirs was indeed a close friendship—so much so that it even led to rumors of impropriety. Once, while she was married to Mel Ferrer, Givenchy and Audrey were photographed coming out of a building with an apartment to let sign. The papers said she was going to leave her husband … in fact she was helping Givenchy find an apartment in Rome.

In an interview with Wanda Hale that appeared in *Motion Picture*, May 1964, she talked about Givenchy:

" 'Still Givenchy?' I asked.

'Of course,' she replied. 'He is the only designer who makes clothes that suit me. In his things I feel well dressed but never overdressed. They are simple and elegant and functional. This black dress I've had three years. It's been made over twice.' "

Elsewhere, she admitted she was always terrified before public functions until she put on "those wonderful garments that Hubert has made me. When I wear them they always take away all my insecurity, all my shyness … so I can talk in front of 800 people."

When she learned she was dying, it was Givenchy who chartered a jet to enable her to return from California to Switzerland. He was one of the pall bearers at her funeral.

"Audrey knew herself perfectly—the qualities as well as the flaws she perceived herself as having. I had not dressed her for a film since she became devoted to UNICEF, but I continued to make some of her evening dresses and day wear. She once told me, 'When I talk about UNICEF in front of the television cameras, I am naturally emotional. Wearing your blouse makes me feel protected.' It was one of the most touching compliments she gave me."
Hubert De Givenchy

ABOVE: Audrey models an emerald green velvet Givenchy evening dress. She sports an emerald and sapphire tiara and opera-length white gloves. *Bettmann/Corbis*

LEFT: Audrey with Hubert de Givenchy at a party for the Givenchy line in Paris. *B.D.V./Corbis*

4 LIFE AT THE TOP 1960–68

"The kind of man I'm attracted to can be tall or short, fair or dark, handsome or homely. Physical good looks don't necessarily appeal to me just by themselves. If a man has that indefinable quality that I can only call 'warmth' or 'charm', then I'll feel at ease with him."
Audrey Hepburn

The 1960s began in the most glorious way for Audrey and her husband when Sean Hepburn Ferrer announced his arrival on January 17, 1960, in Lucerne, Switzerland. The joy and relief of a healthy son was palpable as Hepburn told reporters, "I'm still filled with the wonder of his being, to be able to go out and come back and find that he's still there …"

She would remain at home caring for Sean for three months before returning to work to begin filming what would become her most iconic role. The part of socialite

Holly Golightly in the adaptation of Truman Capote's novella *Breakfast At Tiffany's* was originally intended for Marilyn Monroe, but Hepburn would beat the temperamental diva to the part.

Capote acknowledged the actress born Norma Jeane Mortenson was his desired choice: "Holly had to have something touching about her … unfinished. Marilyn had that." But Hepburn, now 32, was in the prime of her career, while Monroe's would be tragically cut short less than a year after the film's release.

Unwittingly, Audrey inspired Henry Mancini to create his greatest song, "Moon River," for her to sing while perched on a fire escape. "Without Audrey there'd be no 'Huckleberry Friend'," he'd later acknowledge, having written a simple yet somehow sophisticated song that could be played on the white notes of the piano alone. Lyricist Johnny Mercer didn't see the appeal at first, but hundreds of cover versions and an Oscar later he was forced to reassess their creation.

LEFT: Strolling down Via Veneto, Mel and Audrey enjoy the sights October 19, 1961. Mel was in Rome to film *The Black Lancer. Bettmann/ Corbis*

RIGHT: Audrey in 1960s' striped trousers. She would also champion the Breton striped top. *Sunset Boulevard/Corbis*

" 'Moon River' was written for her. No one else has ever understood it so completely. There have been more than a thousand versions of 'Moon River,' but hers is unquestionably the greatest. When we previewed the film, the head of Paramount was there, and he said, 'One thing's for sure. That f***ing song's gotta go.' Audrey shot right up out of her chair! Mel Ferrer had to put his hand on her arm to restrain her. That's the closest I have ever seen her come to losing control."

Henry Mancini (composer, "Moon River")

Breakfast At Tiffany's would not be Audrey's most successful film in box-office terms, but would have a significant cultural impact. Its popularity would grow with each passing year, long after her career had ended, and is now the movie with which she is synonymous.

That made Audrey's next film choice all the more controversial. She was cast as teacher Karen Wright in the remake of Lillian Helman's *The Children's Hour,* a play that caused shockwaves for its homosexual content.

The story saw Audrey's character Karen caught up in a whispering campaign over her relationship with fellow teacher Martha Dobie, played by Shirley MacLaine. Parents quickly remove their children from school upon hearing the two teachers are engaged in a lesbian relationship, and the story ends in tragedy for both women.

LEFT: Barbara Streisand and Audrey meet in New York after a performance of *Funny Girl. Bettmann/Corbis*

RIGHT: Another typical 1960s photo shoot—Audrey holding an orange parasol. *CinemaPhoto/Corbis*

"Audrey was the kind of person who when she saw someone else suffering tried to take their pain on herself. She was a healer. She knew how to love. You didn't have to be in constant contact with her to feel you had a friend. We always picked up right where we left off. She tried to teach me how to dress, and I tried to teach her how to be eloquently profane!"

Shirley MacLaine (costar, *The Children's Hour*)

The play had been previously adapted in 1936 as *These Three,* the lesbian angle disguised as a heterosexual love triangle with one of the teachers accused of seducing the other's fiancé. *The Children's Hour* saw the play's original subject matter restored.

The taboo subject matter was a brave move even for the Sixties, and was a far cry from the mainstream acceptability of *Breakfast At Tiffany's*. But the prospect of a reunion with *Roman Holiday* director William Wyler convinced Hepburn to take on the part.

The film was a critical success, gathering five Oscar nominations though winning none. But the leap into the unknown was a daring career move that paid off; the Hepburn repertoire was expanded and respect was growing apace.

The death of Audrey's dog Famous, a gift from her husband in the early days of their relationship, caused her to relocate to Paris with Sean; Mel was already there, filming World War II epic *The Longest Day*. She deserved some rest and recuperation after rushing back to work soon after giving birth.

RIGHT: Albert Finney and Audrey on set for *Two for the Road* which was shot between May and September 1966. *Sunset Boulevard/Corbis*

ABOVE: Audrey at a party in Paris August 17, 1961. *Mirrorpix*

LEFT: Julie Andrews was passed over for Audrey for the role of Eliza Doolittle in the film *My Fair Lady*, even though she had originated the character on stage. The benefit of this was that it freed her to play the title role in *Mary Poppins*, for which she won the Academy Award for Best Actress; Audrey was not even nominated for *My Fair Lady*. Here the two of them stand after Andrews received her Oscar. April 5, 1965. *Getty Images*

This time out was, however, to be interrupted by contractual obligations. She still had one film left on her Paramount contract, but such was her pulling power that she didn't need to leave the French capital as she began filming *Paris When It Sizzles*.

Filming for the romantic comedy began in July 1962, and Audrey found herself starring alongside William Holden, with whom she had previously worked on *Sabrina*. Holden was then said to have held a flame for Hepburn and she was allegedly concerned about linking up with him again, particularly in a romantic film.

The plot saw Holden star as screenwriter Richard Benson, who leaves writing a script for his boss until just two days before the deadline. Secretary Gabrielle Simpson (Hepburn) is enlisted to do the typing, and romance inevitably ensues.

The film was over-budget and suffered from Holden's alcohol issues. It was subsequently held back by Paramount for two years, finally securing a release in 1964.

No sooner had *Paris* … wrapped than work on a new Parisian-based flick began—one Audrey was more than excited about filming. *Charade* saw her finally team up with Cary Grant in an Alfred Hitchcock-style thriller comedy.

Charade was released at the end of 1963 and became Audrey's most successful film to date, grossing over $6 million. The eventual coming together of two of Hollywood's biggest stars undoubtedly helped the movie's box office performance. "Working with Cary is so easy," Audrey gushed about her co-star after finishing the film. "He does all the acting and I just react."

Filming for *Paris When It Sizzles* and *Charade* took the best part of eight months, and after their completion Hepburn retired to resume her duties as a mother. Perhaps there was only one role that could tempt her back in front of a camera; Hepburn had been quoted as

ABOVE: The BAFTAs on in April 1964: L–R, Rachel Roberts, Audrey, and Dirk Bogarde. *Mirrorpix*

LEFT: Audrey and Mel, April 1964. *Mirrorpix*

saying "I'd do anything to play Eliza Doolittle in *My Fair Lady*." In 1963 her dream came true.

The film was inspired by the enormously successful Broadway production of the same name, and anticipation for the screen version was huge—especially with a budget of $17million. Leading man Rex Harrison remained in the role of phonetics professor Henry Higgins, but the choice to replace his fellow stage star Julie Andrews with Audrey was a controversial one.

Many critics were critical of the choice to drop 28-year-old Andrews, who had helped make the stage show the most successful in history, but rumors of the actress refusing to take a screen test abounded as Audrey was given the nod. The pressure was on to fill Andrews' shoes.

"I understood the dismay of people who had seen Julie on Broadway," Audrey said years later. "[But] if I turned it down they would offer it to another movie actress [and] I thought I was entitled to do it as much as the third girl."

Though her acting would pull in the punters, Audrey's singing was not deemed adequate and her voice was dubbed by famous playback singer Marni Nixon.

The film itself was a rousing success on its release at the tail-end of 1964, winning eight Academy Awards and silencing Hepburn's critics. But the personal battle—if there was one—with Andrews was lost as her rival scooped the Best Actress Oscar in 1965 for her role as Mary Poppins.

All was no longer well on the domestic front. Eight months' time off trying to save her strained marriage to Mel Ferrer preceded work on her next film. Audrey returned to Paris in an attempt to take her mind off events at home, teaming with director William Wyler for the third time as Nicole Bonnet in the comedy *How To Steal A Million*.

ABOVE and RIGHT: Two more views of the 1964 BAFTAs. *Mirrorpix*

Hepburn was cast opposite *Lawrence Of Arabia* star Peter O'Toole as a daughter of an art fraudster who teams up with a crook to steal a fake statue. Working with the Irish actor put the smile back on Audrey's face, even if the film itself fared relatively poorly in the shadow of *My Fair Lady*.

Another miscarriage the same year plunged Audrey into depression, turning down scripts to spend more time with Mel and Sean. But in 1966 she accepted a role in *Two For The Road*, a film that ironically charted the progression of a stale marriage—a case of art imitating life.

"Playing a love scene with a woman as sexy as Audrey, you sometimes get to the edge where make-believe and reality are blurred, all that staring into each other's eyes—you pick up vibes that are decidedly not fantasy ... The time spent with Audrey is one of the closest I've ever had." Albert Finney

Hepburn, 36, played Joanna Wallace, while her husband Mark was played by 30-year-old Albert Finney. The pair got on well, sparking rumors of an affair. The film received a modest reception; its non-linear narrative pushed it just beyond the barriers of the mainstream, but critics hailed Audrey's performance.

LEFT: Audrey as Eliza Doolittle in *My Fair Lady*. *Popperfoto/Getty Images*

RIGHT: The publicity surrounding the release of *My Fair Lady* was massive on both sides of the Atlantic. Here, Audrey arrives for the premiere of *My Fair Lady* in New York with husband Mel Ferrer (L) and Stan Holloway (R) who played her father in the film, October 1964. *Mirrorpix*

She would progress to an even more challenging role, as blind woman Susy Hendrix in *Wait Until Dark*. Hepburn's harrowing and thought-provoking performance in an adaptation of Frederick Knott's stage play gained her an Oscar nomination for Best Actress, but she lost out to another Hepburn—Katharine, for her role of Christina Drayton in *Guess Who's Coming To Dinner*.

Hepburn was taking the praise for her role with a pinch of salt; her marriage to Mel was on the rocks. Another miscarriage midway through 1967 only served to put more pressure on the relationship, and shortly afterward the couple split for good; their divorce was announced at the end of 1968.

Audrey would retain custody of Sean and continued to reside in Switzerland. With no films on the horizon she would enter the 1970s playing the sole role of mother. But she could not hide from love for long; in January she married Italian psychiatrist and playboy Andrea Dotti. They had met on a cruise in the summer of 1968 and immediately fell in love.

At 31, Dotti was nine years Audrey's junior, unusual in her leading men both on and off screen, but the age gap was something that did not bother her. "I had lived longer than Andrea, but it did not mean I was more mature. Intellectually, he was older than I. His work had matured him beyond his years."

It ended a whirlwind of a decade for Audrey, both personally and professionally. Fans around the world were left wondering if she would return to Hollywood or retire gracefully with her son and new husband.

LEFT: Audrey arrives in London from Zurich for the Royal Charity Premiere of *My Fair Lady* at the Warner Theatre, January 19, 1965. *Mirrorpix*

RIGHT: Audrey, Stan Holloway (L) and Rex Harrison (R) at a press reception at the Savoy Hotel after the Royal Charity Premiere. *Mirrorpix*

ABOVE: Dickie Attenborough (for *Guns at Batasi, Seance on a Wet Afternoon*) and Audrey (for *Charade*) show off their 1965 BAFTAs for Best British Actor and Actress. *Mirrorpix*

ABOVE: Fred Zinnemann with Rosalind Russell and Audrey after his double Oscar win for *A Man for All Seasons* in 1966. *Bettmann/Corbis*

Audrey at Heathrow Airport, November 6, 1966. *Mirrorpix*

Audrey on the beach at St. Tropez during shooting of *Two for the Road*. *Terry O'Neill/Getty Images*

AUDREY AND HER CHILDREN

"There is nothing more important to me than having given birth."
Audrey Hepburn

A udrey loved children and desperately wanted her own. She had a close relationship with her mother and dreamed of family life. Finally, after two miscarriages, on July 17, 1960, at the age of 31, Audrey gave birth to Sean. Mel sent her close friend Marie-Louise Habets (Sister Luke in *The Nun's Story*) a telegram:

"BOY SEAN BORN TWO FORTY THIS AFTERNOON NINE POUNDS AUDREY BEATIFICALLY HAPPY LOVE MEL."

She told Sean that his arrival was "the greatest joy for me, because that's all I really wanted in the world." In turn he said, "I suppose people could blame me for ending her career. She knew her potential. If she had kept working, the parts were there for her, and her success professionally would have continued at a high level for years. But she wanted to be with her family. She wanted a private life. And she couldn't bear the thought that she might fail as a mother. It was too important to her."

Initially, she had to continue her career, however, and

LEFT: Audrey, Mel, and Sean in the clinic at Lucerne, July 19, 1960. *STR/ Keystone/Corbis*

RIGHT: Helped by Swiss policemen, Audrey and Andrea Dotti, with Sean between them, make their way through a crowd of newsmen and well-wishers January 18, 1969, following their wedding. *Bettmann/Corbis*

Sean would not see a great deal of her for long periods of time while she was away filming. On top of this, her marriage to Mel Ferrer ended in 1968 and Sean had to come to terms with divorce. But soon Audrey was settled again, with Italian Andrea Dotti, and on February 8, 1970, Audrey's second son, Luca, was born by Caesarean section in Lausanne, Switzerland.

By this time Audrey was 40 and although she would like to have had more children—Andrea Dotti says she "would have loved to have had a larger family"—the doctor advised against it. Instead, Audrey stayed away from films until *Robin And Marian* in 1975. She was able to spend time with her children and do all the normal things—or as normal as one of the world's greatest stars could manage. She could walk Luca to school but the paparazzi followed her everywhere.

Both sons were at her side when she died in 1993 and after her death, Sean, Luca and Robert Wolders founded the Audrey Hepburn Children's Fund to continue providing helping hands to children all over the world.

THE UNFORGIVEN (1960)

Director: John Huston

United Artists

Released April 1960. Technicolor

Burt Lancaster – Ben Zachary

Audrey Hepburn – Rachel Zachary

Audie Murphy – Cash Zachary

John Saxon – Johnny Portugal

Charles Bickford – Zeb Rawlins

Lillian Gish – Mattilda Zachary

Albert Salmi – Charlie Rawlins

Joseph Wiseman – Abe Kelsey

June Walker – Hagar Rawlins

Kipp Hamilton – Georgia Rawlins

Arnold Merritt – Jude Rawlins

Doug McClure – Andy Zachary

Carlos Rivas – Lost Bird

The 1950s' western movies usually had few pretensions: they were adventure stories with white hats and black hats or cowboys and Indians. The 1960s saw a more complicated view of race with different viewpoints—and in *The Unforgiven*, produced right at the start of the decade, John Huston, as *The New York Times* critic Bosley Crowther put it, "who made a 'different' Western in his *The Treasure of Sierra Madre*, has obviously tried to make another." *The Unforgiven* is about racial intolerance concerning Audrey's character, and whether she is a Zachary or a Kiowa. The answer in this film was given when Audrey's character kills her Kiowa brother. Huston was not happy with the film—a view confirmed by poor box-office receipts—and Crowther continued, "as the girl, Audrey Hepburn is a bit too polished, too fragile and civilized among such tough and stubborn types as Burt Lancaster as the man of the family, Lillian Gish as the thin-lipped frontier mother and Audie Murphy as a redskin-hating son."

"In Mexico during the shooting, Audrey made me a gray wool poncho that I still wear every day during the winter. Now I'll never take it off."
Lillian Gish (costar, on Audrey's death)

ABOVE: Audrey and Diablo on location on her return to shooting, March 17, 1960. *Bettmann/Corbis*

LEFT: Audrey gets started on a black cashmere sweater on location at Durango, Mexico. She knitted to relax between scenes. *Archive Photos/Getty Images*

AUDREY BREAKS HER BACK

"I remember when Audrey fell off her horse, the only thing she was worried about was that they get to Mel Ferrer to tell him before the press got word of it. She wasn't concerned about the pain. It was just so that Mel heard first."
Lillian Gish (costar, *The Unforgiven*)

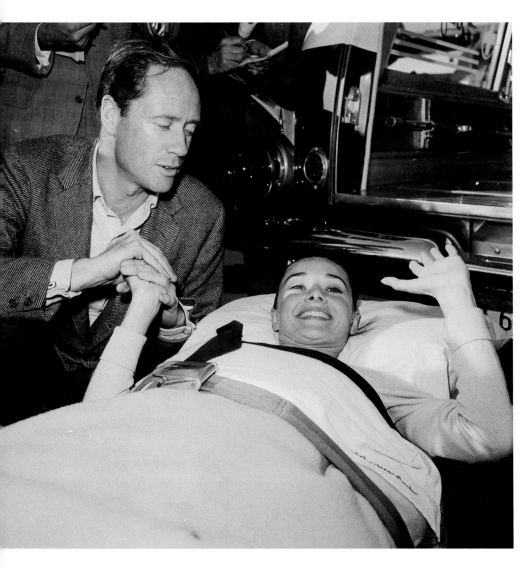

Making films can be tough—particularly westerns, and *The Unforgiven* had its fair share of problems. Audrey's costar, Audie Murphy, while on a duck-hunting trip, had to be rescued after his boat capsized. And Audrey came off her horse, Diablo (Devil), during shooting. Perhaps the horse's name should have given the game away? The damage done to Audrey was severe: four broken vertebrae, torn muscles, and a damaged foot. It would be some weeks before she could start shooting again—and when she did her costumes had to be reworked because she needed an orthopedic brace. Her friend Marie-Louise Habets who Audrey had played in *The Nun's Story*—helped rehabilitate her. All the while she was worried about the health of the child she was carrying—with good reason. Shortly after *The Unforgiven* was completed, Audrey miscarried for the second time. Depressed and inconsolable, when she got pregnant again she refused all work (turning down *West Side Story*) until Sean was born.

LEFT: Audrey smiles on her arrival in Beverley Hills, February 2, 1959. *Bettmann/Corbis*

RIGHT: Mel helps Audrey on her way to a hospital for an X-ray in Beverley Hills, February 26. *Bettmann/Corbis*

BREAKFAST AT TIFFANY'S (1961)

"I dare say all of the men who worked with her fell in love with Audrey. You couldn't help it. She was somebody who comes along whose friendship you cherish." Blake Edwards

Director: Blake Edwards
Paramount Pictures
Released October 1961. Technicolor

Audrey Hepburn – Holly Golightly
George Peppard – Paul "Fred" Varjak
Patricia Neal – 2-E (Mrs Failenson)
Buddy Ebsen – Doc. Golightly
Martin Balsam – O.J. Berman
José Luis de Villalonga – José da Silva Pereira
John McGiver – Tiffany's Salesman

Hepburn's portrayal of Manhattan socialite Holly Golightly in *Breakfast At Tiffany's* would stay with her for the rest of her career, the novel adaptation becoming one of her most successful films.

By now she was at the top of her game professionally, and idolized across the world for her fashion sense and style. It all came together in this Blake Edwards-directed classic.

The film sees Texan girl Golightly in New York chasing money from various rich men in order to support herself, as well as being paid to deliver drug information from an incarcerated mob boss. She meets her new neighbor, struggling writer Paul Varjak (George Peppard), who eventually falls in love with her.

Despite her gold-digging ways, Paul perseveres with his affections and the pair close the film together. The adaptation of Truman Capote's 1958 novella gained multiple plaudits through Hepburn's portrayal of Golightly, a role Capote reportedly intended for Marilyn Monroe.

But while Monroe would be dead less than a year after the film's release, Hepburn was still on the rise; her outfits designed by designer friend Hubert de Givenchy reaffirmed her status as every girl's role model—and every man's dream.

ABOVE and RIGHT: Classic scenes from *Breakfast at Tiffany's. Sunset Boulevard/Corbis* and *Paramount Pictures/Getty Images*

LEFT: Audrey and George Peppard. *Sunset Boulevard/Corbis*   ABOVE: Audrey and Buddy Ebsen on set. *Sunset Boulevard/Corbis*

THE LOUDEST WHISPER (1961)

(The Children's Hour, UK)
Director: William Wyler
United Artists
Released December 1961. Black and white

Audrey Hepburn – Karen Wright
Shirley MacLaine – Martha Dobie
James Garner – Dr. Joe Cardin

*"I've never loved a man. I never knew
why before, maybe it's that."*
(Shirley MacLaine as Martha Dobie)

The film tackled a controversial, and at the time a
forbidden subject, lesbianism. But following its stage
success on Broadway Samuel Goldwyn was interested
in producing the film. The subject matter is alluded
to in the film but never openly expressed.

Based on the story by Lillian Hellman, the
action is set in a New England girls' school where
two teachers Martha and Karen (MacLaine and
Hepburn respectively) are wrongly accused of
lesbianism by a vengeful schoolgirl. Even Karen's
fiancée, Dr. Joe Cardin begins to doubt their
relationship. Eventually the truth comes out, but by
then the damage has been done as Martha realizes
that she really does love Karen, but Karen does not
reciprocate her feelings so Martha hangs herself.

The few critics who reviewed the film were mixed
in their responses, but all praised Audrey's performance.
It was nominated for five Academy Awards and three
Golden Globes. Generally, however, the film was ignored
by filmgoers and critics alike and rather sank without a
trace.

LEFT: Shirley MacLaine as Martha Dobie and Audrey. *John Springer Collection/Corbis*

RIGHT: Student Mary Tilford (left) played by Karen Balkin in a scene with Miriam Hopkins as Lily Mortar, and Audrey as Karen Wright. *John Springer Collection/Corbis*

CHARADE (1963)

Director: Stanley Donen
Universal Studios
Released December 1963. Technicolor

Cary Grant – Peter Joshua
Audrey Hepburn – Regina Lampert
Walter Matthau – Hamilton Bartholemew
James Coburn – Tex Panthollow
George Kennedy – Herman Scobie
Dominique Minot – Sylvie Gaudet
Ned Glass – Leopold W. Gideon

"Paris is always a good idea."
Audrey Hepburn

Charade is a slick and mature thriller/comedy in which Audrey Hepburn finally teams up with suave Hollywood veteran Cary Grant after several near-misses, including 1957's *Love In The Afternoon*.

Hepburn plays Reggie Lampert, who returns home from a ski trip to find her husband murdered. She discovers he was part of a team that stole $250,000 in World War II before double-crossing his fellow criminals and taking all the proceeds for himself.

She comes in contact with Grant's character, one of her late husband's associates involved in the theft. Shifty and aloof, he changes his name throughout the film and openly admits he is after the loot.

The interaction between Hepburn and Grant was praised by critics, despite the 25-year age gap. In the changing world of film, notably the emergence of the Sean Connery-led *James Bond* films, the pair were said to provide a throwback to the Fifties.

Grant would only make two more films before retiring from movies, passing away in 1986. *Charade* would provide Audrey with a successful reunion with *Funny Face* director Stanley Donen, her reward a third Best Actress BAFTA.

LEFT and ABOVE: Audrey won a BAFTA for her performance in *Charade. Getty Images; CinemaPhoto/Corbis*

PARIS WHEN IT SIZZLES (1964)

Director: Richard Quine
Paramount Pictures
Released April 1964. Technicolor

William Holden – Richard Benson
Audrey Hepburn – Gabrielle Simpson
Grégoire Asian – Police Inspector Gilet
Noël Coward – Alexander Meyerheim

"I remember the day I arrived at Orly Airport . . . just like a condemned man walking the last mile. I realized that I had to face Audrey and I had to deal with my drinking. And I didn't think I could handle either situation." **William Holden**

A lighthearted rom-com with a musical score by Nelson Riddle the plot revolves around a playboy screenwriter suffering from writers block who puts off writing his script until two days before presenting it to the producer Alexander Meyerheim. Gabrielle Simpson is the hired temp with whom he bounces ideas around in an attempt to come up with the plot for the screenplay "The Girl Who Stole The Eiffel Tower." As they work together they inevitably fall in love.

In actual fact the atmosphere while making the film was difficult as Holden was still drinking heavily and still in love with Audrey; he didn't want to make the film but he was contractually obliged to—as was Audrey. In fact Richard Quine sent Holden away for a week's alcohol treatment during filming. Holden also tried, without success, to rekindle her feelings for him. For her part Audrey insisted on having dressing room number 55—the number she had for *Roman Holiday* and *Breakfast at Tiffany's*—and insisted on the dismissal of cinematographer Claude Renoir who she felt was not sympathetically shooting her. She also insisted on a perfume credit for Givenchy!

In uncredited performances, Mel Ferrer plays a party guest, Tony Curtis a policeman, and Marlene Dietrich appears as herself. The critics almost universally panned the film for the absurd storyline but commended the principals working against the odds.

ABOVE: Audrey in the role of Gabrielle Simpson. *Popperfoto/Getty Images*

LEFT: William Holden and Audrey cruise along the Seine. *Getty Images*

MY FAIR LADY (1965)

Director: George Cukor
Warner Brothers Pictures
Released January 1965. Technicolor

Audrey Hepburn – Eliza Doolittle
Rex Harrison – Prof. Henry Higgins
Stanley Holloway – Alfred P. Doolittle
Wilfrid Hyde-White – Colonel Hugh Pickering
Gladys Cooper – Mrs. Higgins
Jeremy Brett – Freddy Eynsford-Hill

"I understood the dismay of people who had seen Julie on Broadway. Julie made that role her own, and for that reason I didn't want to do the film when it was first offered. But Jack Warner never wanted to put Julie in the film. He was totally opposed to it, for whatever reason. Then I learned that if I turned it down, they would offer it to still another movie actress. So I felt I should have the same opportunity to play it as any other film actress." **Audrey Hepburn**

An adaptation of an adaptation, *My Fair Lady* survived any accusations of becoming diluted by becoming one of Audrey Hepburn's most successful films, raking in eight Academy awards.

The popular story of young Cockney sparrow Eliza Doolittle being transformed into a lady of the upper class by a phonetics professor proved to be a successful role for Hepburn, despite some critics' misgivings.

Professor Henry Higgins, played by Rex Harrison, believed he could pass any lady of a lower class off as a duchess if only he could teach them the "Queen's English." The film was directed by George Cukor, no stranger to stage adaptations having already headed *The Philadelphia Story* and *Born Yesterday* in 1940 and 1950 respectively.

The film and its soundtrack, which included hits like "Wouldn't It Be Loverly" and "On The Street Where You Live," proved popular with fans, and was nominated for a mammoth twelve Oscars, winning eight of them, including best costume design—unsurprising, really, for an Audrey Hepburn film.

By the age of 35 Audrey had starred in over twenty motion pictures, but her workrate would slow in the coming years.

ABOVE: The classic Ascot scene: front row L–R, Isobel Elsom, Gladys Cooper, Jeremy Brett, Audrey, Rex Harrison, and Wilfrid Hyde-White. *Underwood & Underwood/Corbis*

RIGHT: Audrey as Eliza Doolittle at Ascot when Rex Harrison as Professor Henry Higgins takes her to his mother's box at the racecourse. *Bettmann/Corbis; Sunset Boulevard/Corbis*

HOW TO STEAL A MILLION (1966)

Director: William Wyler
20th Century Fox
Released August 1966. Color

Audrey Hepburn – Nicole Bonnet
Peter O'Toole – Simon Dermott
Eli Wallach – Davia Leland
Hugh Griffith – Charles Bonnet
Charles Boyer – DeSolnay

"Having a wonderful crime! Wish you were here!" Tagline

In this comedy heist movie Nicole Bonnet (Audrey) is the daughter of a respected art collector, but in reality she and his father are both art forgers. When his supposed Benvenuto Cellini statuette of Venus (sculpted by grandfather) is lent to a museum—against Nicole's better judgment—it soon becomes clear that they will be exposed and sent to prison. As chance would have it gentleman art thief Simon Dermott is caught by Nicole stealing one of their paintings and she soon persuades him to help her steal the sculpture before the mandatory authenticity test. During the successful heist they fall in love but afterward Dermott reveals that he is in reality an art fraud private investigator but he will not expose her father if he promises to give up forging paintings. He agrees and the young couple are free to completely fall in love and marry. Throughout the film Audrey is elegantly swathed in Givenchy.

The critics loved the film despite its whimsicality, *The New York Times* said, "It may all be deception … It is still a delightful lot of flummery while it is going on, especially the major, central business of burglarizing the museum."

RIGHT: Peter O'Toole and Audrey made a charismatic couple. *Sunset Boulevard/Corbis*

TWO FOR THE ROAD (1967)

Director: Stanley Donen
20th Century Fox
Released: April 1967. Color

Audrey Hepburn – Joanne Wallace
Albert Finney – Mark Wallace
Eleanor Bron – Cathy Maxwell-Manchester
William Daniels – Howard Maxwell-Manchester

The story follows twelve years of marriage between architect Mark Wallace and his wife Jo(anne) with a theme song composed by Henry Mancini. Mostly set while traveling to and around the south of France the story jumps backward and forward in time with six different stories charting the milestones and difficulties in their marriage—a quite experimental concept for the period. The movie starts with Jo flying to join Mark in the south of France. On the plane she recalls their marriage in various episodes from their time together in a jumbled up chronology starting with when they first met when she was a music student and he a struggling young architect. The film ends with their problems resolved when they both realize that despite having extra-martial affairs they both actually love each other and want to be together. They then drive off into a new life in Italy. *The New York Times* critic summed it up, "there are some precious moments of romantic charm in this bitter account of domestic discord amid surroundings that should inspire nothing but delight. And so one must seize upon them for the entertainment that is to be had, and endure the tedium of much of the picture." Off screen though, this was a happy shoot with the director saying that Audrey was freer and happier than he had ever seen her and he put much of this down to working with Finney.

"At the cast party every male member of the crew—and there were two crews, one English, one French—wanted to dance with her. She danced until she had blisters on her feet. She must have been exhausted—but she made sure they all got their dance."
William Daniels (costar)

ABOVE: Audrey Hepburn and Albert Finney slosh around happily during the filming of a swimming pool sequence at St. Tropez, July 8, 1966. Luckily, the shooting of the swimming sequences coincided with soaring temperatures. *Terry O'Neill/Getty Images*

LEFT: Audrey in pensive mood by the swimming pool on location in St Tropez. *Terry O'Neill/Getty Images*

WAIT UNTIL DARK (1967)

Director: Terence Young
Warner Brothers Pictures
Released May 1967. Technicolor

Audrey Hepburn – Susy Hendrix
Alan Arkin – Roat/Roat Jr./Roat Sr.
Richard Crenna – Mike Talman
Efrem Zimbalist Jr. – Sam Hendrix
Jack Weston – Carlino
Samantha Jones – Lisa
Julie Herrod – Gloria

Wait Until Dark was another transfer
from stage to screen, and this crime
thriller from Broadway proved to be
another smash hit. Hepburn threw
critics another curveball by turning in
a mesmerizing performance in a tough
genre.

Original playwright Frederick
Knott had seen his earlier thriller *Dial M For Murder*
successfully adapted by Alfred Hitchcock in 1954, so hopes
were high. Confidence in the film's success was boosted with
the appointment of James Bond director Terence Young.

Hepburn shines in her portrayal of Susy Hendrix, a
young woman blinded in a car accident. Her husband Sam,
played by Efrem Zimbalist Jr., is asked to carry a doll over the
Canadian/US border—but the toy is stuffed with drugs and the
discovery kicks off a horrible ordeal for both Susy and Sam.

Hepburn's showing was recognized in the form of three
Best Actress nominations but, amazingly, she failed to pick up
either a Laurel, Golden Globe, or an Oscar. She would not
make another motion picture for nearly a decade.

*"[Audrey] trained extensively beforehand
at a nearby institute for the blind, and is
remarkably convincing. She deserved her
Academy Award nomination for the role
…"* **Filmfanatic.org**

ABOVE: Richard Crenna as Mike Talman, Audrey as Suzy
Hendrix, and Jack Weston as Carlino. *Bettmann/Corbis*

RIGHT: Hepburn even learned to read Braille as she played a blind
girl. *Getty Images*

HOUSEWIFE
AND MOTHER 1969–80

"My goal was not to have huge luxuries. As a child, I wanted a house with a garden, which I have today. This is what I dreamed of. I'd never worry about age if I knew I could go on being loved and having the possibility to love. If I'm old and my husband doesn't want me, or my children think me ugly and do not want me – that would be a tragedy. So it isn't age or even death that one fears, as much as loneliness and the lack of affection." Audrey Hepburn

The 1970s began almost identically to the previous decade, with Audrey giving birth at the beginning of the year. On February 8, 1970, her second child, Luca Dotti, was born by Caesarean section in Lausanne, Switzerland and was doted on as any new arrival inevitably is. But while it was an undoubtedly happy occasion, the cracks were already beginning to show in her marriage to Andrea.

Rumors of infidelity dogged the psychiatrist, but he protested his innocence to Audrey and the couple stayed together. Remembering her own father's departure from her life—"I lived in constant fear of being left," she later said of her married life— she seemed determined to hang on to her man even if it was at the cost of her self-respect.

The star that once graced billboards and movies across the world was now settling into the role of a housewife and mother in Rome—and, for the most part, she claimed to love it. "It's sad if people think [it's] a dull existence, [but] you can't just buy an apartment and furnish it and walk away. It's the flowers you choose, the music you

ABOVE: Audrey returning from shopping, while she was living in Rome with her husband, Dr. Andrea Dotti, April 3, 1971. *Bettmann/Corbis*

AFFITTASI
APPARTAMENTO

Audrey with mother-in-law Signora Paolo Bandini on a house-hunting excursion, 1969. *Time & Life Pictures/Getty Images*

play, the smile you have waiting. I want it to be gay and cheerful, a haven in this troubled world." In 1988 she said, "I had to make a choice at one point in my life, of missing films or missing my children. It was a very easy decision to make because I missed my children so very much. When my elder son started going to school, I could not take him with me any more and that was tough for me, so I stopped accepting pictures. I withdrew to stay home with my children. I was very happy. It is not as if I was sitting at home, frustrated, biting my nails."

Yet it was still in Switzerland where she felt truly safe from that world, and it was a sticking point that Andrea was reluctant to leave his Roman practice to relocate. She was turning down countless scripts to stay at home with Luca and Sean, now ten.

> ### "Whatever happens, the most important thing is growing old gracefully. And you can't do that on the cover of a fan magazine." Audrey Hepburn

Her fans were growing restless and wanted their idol to return, but Audrey was unapologetic. "I've never believed in 'God-given talent'," she protested. "I adored my work and I did my best. But I don't think I'm robbing anyone of anything."

It was during this self-imposed exile from the screen that Audrey first began working with children's charity UNICEF, a relationship that would last until her death. She appeared on a Christmas television special titled *A World Of Love*, where she documented the children's charity's efforts in Italy.

She was happy to be away from movies and Hollywood, which she said was all "sex and violence," something she wanted to shield her sons from with Sean now a teenager and Luca entering school.

ABOVE and LEFT: Audrey growing old gracefully in 1975. *Pictorial Parade/Archive Photos/Getty Images*; *Douglas Kirkland/Corbis*

It would take a special film and a special cast to bring Audrey out of retirement, and that film would be *Robin And Marian*. She would star alongside Sean Connery in the comedy about legendary rogue Robin Hood's later life with his love Maid Marian. The casting of Connery proved a decisive factor in her return: "[Sean and Luca] begged me to do the film. They were so thrilled at the idea of meeting James Bond."

"Having known Audrey, I have less tolerance for the star thing, and she was responsible for me having less tolerance—if Audrey Hepburn can live on the road for three months, and be more talented than 99.9 percent of anybody on this planet, and come in and be on time and know her material and be delightful and professional and give you gold on camera—when I come across the behaviour now, I have a really hard time with it. Celebrities today need to go to the Audrey Hepburn School of How to Be a Star. She should have given lessons or written a book about it!" **Julie Leifermann**

She filmed in Spain and brought her sons with her, before the film was released in March 1976. A US publicity blitz may have reminded Audrey why she left it all behind, but her fans and peers gave her a rapturous welcome, hoping the return would not be short-lived. But her husband, not as fond of the home life as she, featured in the papers in the company of younger women and, just as with Mel Ferrer, cracks were starting to appear in their marriage. Even so, Andrea was at her side at the 1976 Academy Awards where Audrey presented an Oscar to Michael Douglas for *One Flew Over The Cuckoo's Nest*.

RIGHT: Back in the Hollywood spotlight, Audrey is shown participating in the Academy Awards Ceremonies March 29, 1976. *Bettmann/Corbis*

Her growing fears about Rome and its security prompted her to move Sean and Luca back to Switzerland, flying to Rome to see Andrea, who still refused to relocate. The stress was none the more evident when Audrey suffered another miscarriage at the age of 45. (Her problems in carrying children to term were, she would later explain, even more of a blight on her life than her parents' divorce.)

Having turned down offers, including *A Bridge Too Far*, she finally agreed to star in the thriller *Bloodline*. Her choice of movie was based on money-to-work ratio and close proximity to her sons, but it didn't make for a good career move; *Bloodline,* adapted from a trashy Sidney Sheldon novel, was to be her only R-rated film. Audrey had abandoned her principles in order to continue supporting her sons.

She had linked up with *Wait Until Dark* director Terence Young, perhaps feeling a debt to him for her leading role in that 1960s film. But the risqué plot and scenes made a near 50-year-old Hepburn uncomfortable, and the film was duly panned by critics, the *New York Daily News* reporting "*Bloodline* offers the chance to see Hepburn on screen again … but what rotten circumstances."

Circumstances at home were not much better, and in 1980 Audrey split with Andrea Dotti; his wayward behavior proved too much for Hepburn, whose patience and understanding throughout the last decade had finally run out.

Having outgrown the glitz and glamor of Hollywood, and feeling uncomfortable about the lengths actors and directors would go to in creating a successful movie, there were question marks over Audrey's continuing career as she entered the 1980s. She had nothing to prove—would she continue trying?

ABOVE: Audrey presents an Honorary Award to American director, screenwriter, and producer King Vidor at the 51st Academy Awards, April 9, 1979. *Jim McHugh/Sygma/Corbis; Bettmann/Corbis*

ABOVE: Andrea Dotti with Audrey shortly after Police reported that three men tried to kidnap him, February 1976. *Gamma-Keystone via Getty Images*

AUDREY AND DOTTI

"I was no angel—Italian husbands have never been famous for being faithful."
Andrea Dotti

They met cruising around the Greek Islands, and it was a whirlwind romance. A well-off psychiatrist, a few weeks after her divorce from Mel was final, Audrey and Andrea married in Tolochenaz-sur-Morges, on January 18, 1969. Audrey wore a simple pink wool dress and matching scarf designed by her friend, Hubert de Givenchy. Just over a year later, on February 8, 1970, their son Luca was born. Audrey had been very careful during her pregnancy—she was, after all, forty with a track record of miscarriages—and spent some time convalescing after the caesarean. She hoped for more children, but did not, suffering another miscarriage in 1974.

The marriage started well. Dotti obviously loved Hepburn and—a great help—was liked by Sean, who said he was "fun." They lived in Rome where Audrey attempted a normal life, in spite of the unwelcome attentions of the paparazzi. Italy in the mid-1970s was a violent place and in the end the threat of kidnappings—her husband was lucky to escape one attempt with seven stitches to a wound in the head—led her to move back with her two sons to La Paisable. Her husband continued to practice in Rome—but his roving eye provided the paparazzi with an easy target.

The marriage lasted thirteen years and when she felt that the children could cope, the couple divorced. Audrey, said Robert Wolders, "was humiliated. It was especially painful for her to have a second marriage fail." However, unlike Mel Ferrer, with whom Audrey passed few words after their divorce, Andrea Dotti maintained an amicable contact with the household. He never remarried and continued his teaching and practice until his death in 2007.

ABOVE: Audrey and her new husband, Dr. Andrea Dotti, face reporters after their wedding at the townhall in Morges, Switzerland, January 18, 1969. *Bettmann/Corbis*

LEFT and ABOVE: Audrey and Andrea at the 48th Annual Academy Awards ceremony at the Dorothy Chandler Pavilion, Los Angeles, March 22, 1976. *Hulton Archive/Getty Images; Frank Edwards/Fotos International/Hulton Archive/Getty Images*

RIGHT: Audrey's passport shows both Ferrer and Dotti surnames. It's on display at the Audrey In Rome Exhibition, October 25, 2011. *Ernesto Ruscio/Getty Images*

ROBIN AND MARIAN (1976)

Director: Richard Lester
Columbia Pictures
Released July 1976. Technicolor

Sean Connery – Robin Hood
Audrey Hepburn – Lady Marian
Robert Shaw – Sheriff of Nottingham
Richard Harris – Richard the Lionheart
Nicol Williamson – Little John
Denholm Elliott – Will Scarlett
Kenneth Haigh – Sir Ranulf
Ronnie Barker – Friar Tuck

"We arranged the shooting to accommodate her younger son's school holidays, which was very important to her because she was concerned that she spend as much time with him as possible." **Richard Lester** (director, *Robin And Marian*)

Audrey Hepburn made a triumphant return to cinema in her first role for nine years, portraying one of film's most famous characters, Maid Marian, opposite Sean Connery as Robin Hood.

The two veterans of the silver screen performed together for the first time; Hepburn's screen career spoke for itself, while Connery, the original James Bond, had enjoyed success as part of the franchise in *You Only Live Twice* and *Thunderball,* to name just two.

The film is a take on Robin Hood and Marian two decades after their pomp (Connery and Hepburn were both in their mid-forties). Robin had returned from the crusades to be reunited with Marian, but she had turned to religion. Relations thaw after he rescues her from the Sheriff of Nottingham. However the plot ends in tragedy for the pair.

Director Richard Lester was famed for his work with the Beatles in their 1960s films *A Hard Day's Night* and *Help!*. But while the Beatles were young men who brought in audiences, a film about an aging hero brought only moderate success.

The subject-matter was perhaps apt; it would be Hepburn's penultimate movie lead, with only the role of Angela Niotes in 1981's *They All Laughed* to follow.

LEFT: Sean Connery and Audrey enjoyed filming together in Pamplona, Spain. *Douglas Kirkland/Corbis*

RIGHT: Audrey on the set of *Robin and Marian. Douglas Kirkland/Corbis*

BLOODLINE (1979)

Director: Terence Young
Released: June 1979. Color Paramount Pictures

Audrey Hepburn – Elizabeth Roffe
Ben Gazzara – Rhys Williams
James Mason – Sir Alec Nichols
Romy Schneider – Hélène Roffe-Martin
Omar Sharif – Ivo Palazzi

> *"She had a quality no other actress had: a curious combination of lady and pixie. She was a joy to work with—enormous talent and no ego."*
>
> **Sidney Sheldon** (writer, *Bloodline*)

Set among the international jet set with an international cast, the film shows what happens when Elizabeth Roffe inherits her father's multi-billion dollar pharmaceuticals empire after an apparent climbing accident. As the investigation into the exact circumstances of his death progress, the other board members maneuver for power and Elizabeth marries chief CEO Rhys Williams. It emerges that her father was murdered and the suspects include most close members of the family, the board members and even Elizabeth's new husband. Everyone except her wants to sell their shares and go public, her life is in jeopardy and several attempt are made to kill her: she doesn't know who she can trust. A sub plot about the murder of prostitutes and snuff movies does nothing to add to the film which was a critical and box office flop. In a damning review *The New York Times* said, "*Bloodline* takes Miss Hepburn's Givenchy clothes more seriously than it does the actress who wears them, not always becomingly. Under these circumstances, there's no reason to comment on the quality of the individual performances."

RIGHT: The stars of *Bloodline*; L–R—Omar Sharif, Irene Papas, James Mason, Audrey, Ben Gazzara, Romy Schneider, and Maurice Ronet. *Sunset Boulevard/Corbis*

UNICEF AMBASSADOR 1980–93

"After looking inside an insane asylum, visiting a leper colony, talking to missionary workers, and watching operations, I felt very enriched. I developed a new kind of inner peacefulness. A calmness. Things that once seemed so important weren't important any longer."
Audrey Hepburn

ABOVE: Hubert De Givenchy escorts Audrey to the Givenchy 30th anniversary tribute at the Fashion Institute of Technology, 1982. *Bettmann/Corbis*

With her marriage to Andrea Dotti now officially ended, Audrey had already met Dutch actor Robert Wolders with whom she shared many mutual interests. And she was to rely on his support in 1980 as she flew to Dublin where her father was dying.

"Audrey sensed very early in her life and career that self-worth based on fame or beauty is very short-lived, and so she remained forever herself—realistic, aware, and caring." **Robert Wolders**

As has been recounted, her father cut ties with the family after his divorce from Ella and was imprisoned during World War II as a Nazi sympathizer. Audrey had traced him to Dublin with the help of the Red Cross in 1959 and, after visiting him for a first time, had sent him regular funds. They were reconciled before his death, even though his views ran contrary to her own experiences.

Her beloved mother Ella would follow in August 1984, at the age of 84. Audrey was inconsolable: "I was lost without my mother. She had been my sounding

Audrey photographed in Claridges, London in 1989. *Martyn Goddard/Corbis*

board, my conscience. She was not the most affectionate person—in fact there were times when I thought she was cold—but she loved me in her heart, and I knew that all along."

Audrey's last starring role in a movie had come in 1981 with the Peter Bogdanovich-directed *They All Laughed*. She was one of a trio of women (Patti Hansen and Dorothy Stratten playing the others) who fall for the detectives assigned to follow them by their suspicious husbands. The final curtain came six years later in the shape of a poorly received television movie, *Love Among Thieves,* in which she appeared opposite Richard Wagner—an equally low-key end to a stellar acting career. But there were now more important priorities in her life.

The year of 1985 had brought happy news as Audrey's son Sean married; the reception brought her back together with Mel, whom she had not seen for seventeen years. Three years later she was appointed Goodwill Ambassador for the United Nations Children's Fund (UNICEF), an organization she'd previously helped with fundraising events. With both sons now living away—Luca having chosen to live with his father in Rome—she was to devote herself more fully to this work, and it would be the main focus of the rest of her life.

"There is no doubt that the princess did become a queen—not only on the screen. One of the most loved, one of the most skillful, one of the most intelligent, one of the most sensitive, charming actresses—and friends, in my life—but also in the later stages of her life, the UNICEF ambassador to the children of the world. The generosity, sensitivity, the nobility of her service to the children of the world and the mothers of the world will never be forgotten." Gregory Peck

RIGHT: "I like the idea of growing old gracefully and full of wrinkles ... like Audrey Hepburn." Natalie Imbruglia. *Mirrorpix*

When UNICEF lost their ambassador on the death of Danny Kaye in 1987, Audrey immediately agreed to fill the gap. She'd never been comfortable with public acclaim and, while admitting that publicity for her good deeds was embarrassing, "I'm glad I've got a name because I'm using it for all it's worth."

While Hepburn's charity work won the publicity UNICEF desired, there were those who called her "Saint Teresa in designer jeans." But the heartbreaking sights of suffering she witnessed had taken a toll on her. And when she herself suffered excruciating stomach pains while in Somalia it appeared she might be taking things too far. As it turned out, this was the first sign of the cancer that was to claim her life.

> **"Once she sensed that she could trust somebody, she'd do anything for them. And if she were disappointed in them, it would be the end of the world for her."**
> **Robert Wolders**

When not on the road doing charitable work, Audrey found pleasure in a simple home life. Even though she never tied the knot with Rob Wolders, two unhappy marriages being two too many, she was clearly content. "As a child I wanted a house with a garden, which I have today—this is what I dreamed of," stating that her ideal evening was the company of her man and two sons plus "good food and great television." She also said to *USA Today* in 1987, "I'm not a born actress … but I care about expressing feelings, and it's more fun to express happy feelings than tears and pain."

The final curtain came on January 30, 1993, four months before her sixty-fourth birthday, when Audrey Hepburn died at home in her sleep. She was buried in the cemetery at Tolochenaz-sur-Morges; Pastor Maurice Eindiguer, who had married Hepburn and Mel Ferrer

ABOVE: Still beautiful in her sixties. *B.D.V./Corbis*

LEFT: "I have learnt how to live … how to be in the world and of the world, and not just to stand aside and watch." *Adam Knott/Corbis*

thirty-nine years earlier, presided over the funeral. Sean Ferrer said, "Even on the day she died, her thoughts were with the children. She rallied for the last time and wanted to know if there had been any messages from UNICEF about the children in Somalia. Mummy believed in love. She left us with peace."

"If my world were to cave in tomorrow, I would look back on all the pleasures, excitements and worthwhilenesses I have been lucky enough to have had. Not the sadness, not my miscarriages or my father leaving home, but the joy of everything else. It will have been enough." Audrey Hepburn

RIGHT: A picture dated 11 June 11, 1991, shows Elizabeth Taylor (L) and Audrey posing for a photograph as they attend the Charity Dinner "Art against AIDS" in Basel, Switzerland. *EPA/STR Database/Corbis*

ABOVE: American cinema pays tribute to Sean Connery July 24, 1992 *Frank Trapper/Sygma/Corbis*

RIGHT: Audrey in June 1992, some six months before her death. *Helene Bamberger/Gamma-Rapho via Getty Images*

AUDREY AND ROBERT WOLDERS

"I asked her how do you and Rob do it? How do you spend all this time together, travel together, live together, without killing each other? She said, 'We just enjoy going through the world together.' It was the sweetest thing to see their little jokes — that playful, mischievous side of her. She was so smart, so well-read, spoke gazillions of languages. No wonder Robbie never got bored with her." Julie Leifermann

From 1980 until her death, Audrey was attached to Dutch actor Robert Wolders. They had first met in 1979 at a dinner party arranged by Connie Wald, an old friend of Audrey's, after the death of Robert's wife, film star Merle Oberon. They met again in New York while Audrey was filming Peter Bogdanovich's *They All Laughed*. After Audrey's divorce from Dotti was finalized, Wolders became her constant companion, although they never married. In 1989, she said the nine years she had spent with him were the happiest years of her life. "We met at a time when we each had gone through trials, but we knew exactly what we wanted—togetherness," he said.

They lived together in Rome and at La Paisible, and Robert—she called him Robbie—accompanied her to film events and on all her grueling UNICEF tours … and she ventured back into showbusiness as much for the money as any glory—she received $450,000 from Steven Spielberg's *Always* for three days' work. There is no doubt that she was completely happy with Robert.

Robert was there when she died, was a pall bearer, and helped Sean and Luca set up the Audrey Hepburn charity, which he continues to assist. In 1999 he said, "In the six years since she is gone I have become ever more aware of how many lives Audrey touched. I am moved to find that

to many she is a reflection of what we hold most dear; kindness, generosity, charity and humility. People loved her for the right reasons, and she was deserving of that love. I consider myself blessed to have been allowed to discover how deep her soul was in its total commitment to life."

In May 2002 at the UNICEF headquarters in New York, a seven-foot tall bronze sculpture dedicated to Audrey—commissioned and donated by Robert—was unveiled. "Audrey personified the spirit of UNICEF," Wolders said, "and we hope those who see this statue will be inspired by her efforts on behalf of children."

ABOVE: Audrey and Robert. June 12, 1991. *James Andanson/Sygma/Corbis*

LEFT: Audrey and her companion, Robert Wolders, during a winter vacation at Gstaad, December 23, 1982. *James Andanson/Sygma/Corbis*

ALWAYS (1989)

Director: Steven Spielberg
Universal-United Artists
Released December 1989. Panavision

Richard Dreyfuss – Pete Sandich
Holly Hunter – Dorinda Durston
Brad Johnson – Ted Baker
John Goodman – Al Yackey
Audrey Hepburn – Hap

This was Audrey's final film appearance in little more
than a cameo role. Not long into the film and on his
last mission as a firefighting pilot Pete Sandich, always
a reckless daredevil flier, is killed. But he has led an
essentially good life and ascends to Heaven where he
meets Hap (Audrey) an angel. She instructs him to pass
on his aeronautical know-how to Ted Baker, his young
and inexperienced replacement whose mind he is able
to influence. In fact, Audrey has very little screen time
but what she did was praised. Devastated at his loss, his
girlfriend Dorinda slowly gets closer to Ted and gradually
the pair fall in love, a situation that the spectral Pete at
first finds difficult to handle. The film is a virtual remake
of the 1943 *A Guy Named Joe* and was described by *The
New York Times* as "a wonderful Steven Spielberg film
about love and hope and sacrifice, a film in which the
miraculous and the ordinary go hand in hand."

RIGHT: Richard Dreyfuss and Audrey on the set of *Always. Sunset
Boulevard/Corbis*

"She was the best that we could possibly be; she was perfectly charming and perfectly loving. She was a dream. And she was the kind of dream that you remember when you wake up smiling."

Richard Dreyfuss

THEY ALL LAUGHED (1981)

Director: Peter Bogdanovich
20th Century Fox
Released 1981. Color

Audrey Hepburn – Angela Niotes
Ben Gazzara – John Russo
Patti Hansen – Sam
John Ritter – Charles Rutledge
Dorothy Stratten – Dolores Martin

"She did not overdress. She was rather subdued in what she wore. She had this air of the princess. When you've got it, you don't need much. I never heard a vulgar word come out of Audrey. I never heard anyone be vulgar in front of Audrey."

Ben Gazzara (costar, *Bloodline* and *They All Laughed*)

The last of Audrey's lead role films, this is a rom-com set in New York City that revolves around the Odyssey Detective Agency where suspicious clients commission them to follow possibly unfaithful lovers and wives. The plot is a complicated network of love and spying. Audrey is Anglea Niotes, the wife of a wealthy Italian industrialist; she is followed by lothario John Russo, inevitably he falls for her. Audrey's son Sean Ferrer plays a small role as one of the characters, Jose.

The film itself was completely overshadowed by the murder of onetime Playmate, aspiring actress and current girlfriend of Bogdanovich, Dorothy Stratten, by her jealous ex-husband shortly after filming ended. The film is dedicated to her and was released after her death but largely ignored by both the public and critics. Vincent Canby in *The New York Times* commented, "Would that anybody could laugh ... Any way you look at it—as a comedy, as moviemaking, as a financial investment, *They All Laughed* is an immodest disaster." He was kinder about Audrey, "whom Mr. Bogdanovich treats so shabbily that if this were a marriage instead of a movie, she'd have grounds for immediate divorce."

ABOVE: Audrey and director Peter Bogdanovich during filming. *Steve Schapiro/Corbis*

GARDENS OF THE WORLD WITH AUDREY HEPBURN (1993)
AUDREY HEPBURN: IN HER OWN WORDS

Director: Bruce Franchini
PSP TV documentary
First broadcast January 1993. Color

Narrated by Audrey Hepburn, Michael York, Gustavo Tavares

"She never considered herself a good gardener. She liked to talk about how good she was at pulling weeds. But that's because she was just so modest."
Janis Blackschleger (executive producer of the PBS program
Gardens of the World with Audrey Hepburn)

Audrey's last public entertainment project was an ambitious look at gardens filmed on location in public and private gardens in seven different countries—the United States, England, Japan, France, Italy, the Netherlands, and Santo Domingo—in spring and summer 1990. It was the only TV series she appeared in and was not shown until March 1991, after her death. When Audrey fell ill Michael York became the narrator. The original series was in eight 30-minute episodes and based on the book *Gardens of the World* by Penelope Hobhouse and Elvin McDonald, for which Audrey wrote the foreword. To sum up she wrote, "Perhaps if we now take a closer look at our gardens we will better understand how to find a way to save our lovely earth. Have we not lost sight of our only source of life? Or have we at last awakened to the fragility of our beautiful planet?"

The first six episodes were broadcast in 1993 but the final two were delayed until 1996. Audrey donated her fee for the series to UNICEF.

Audrey was posthumously awarded the 1993 Outstanding Individual Achievement Emmy – Informal Programming for her work on the series.

AUDREY AND UNICEF

"People in Ethiopia, the Sudan, etc. don't know Audrey Hepburn, but they recognize the name UNICEF. When they see UNICEF, their faces light up, because they know that something is happening. In the Sudan, for example, they call a water pump 'UNICEF'."

ABOVE: Audrey's first mission for UNICEF was to Ethiopia. *Bettmann/Corbis*

UNICEF—the UN International Children's Emergency Fund—was set up at the end of 1946 to help children in countries that had been devastated by World War II. In 1953 it changed its name to the UN Children's Fund and has continued to provide aid to children and mothers ever since. Its mission statement says: "UNICEF is mandated by the United Nations General Assembly to advocate for the protection of children's rights, to help meet their basic needs and to expand their opportunities to reach their full potential."

One of UNICEF's tools in this struggle is the use of famous people to help publicize and advance their goals—the Special and Goodwill Ambassadors. Audrey had been involved with UNICEF for some time before she was named UNICEF Special Ambassador on March 9, 1988, having participated in fund-raising and advocacy activities, and appeared at benefit events in Tokyo and Macao. She joined a distinguished group of celebrity supporters including Peter Ustinov, Liv Ullmann, Tetsuko Kuroyanagi, Harry Belafonte, and Sir Richard Attenborough. The longest-serving Goodwill Ambassador was Danny Kaye who died in 1987, after 35 years of international humanitarian service to UNICEF and children. At the press conference

announcing her post, Audrey said, "I can testify to what UNICEF means to children because I was among the recipients of food and medical relief right after World War II. I have a long-lasting gratitude and trust for what UNICEF does." Announcing her appointment, UNICEF Executive Director, James P. Grant said, "We are indeed fortunate that people of renown, like Audrey Hepburn, with huge talents, are prepared to give so generously of their time and energies. During recent ad hoc missions for UNICEF … she has demonstrated her remarkable talents as an advocate for children."

Audrey believed that the rich were obliged to help the poor: "Since the world has existed, there has been injustice. But it is one world, the more so as it becomes smaller, more accessible. There is just no question that there is a moral obligation for those who have, to give to those who have nothing."

Her first mission—March 14–18, 1988—was to visit drought-stricken Ethiopia, Africa's poorest country that had endured years of drought-induced famine (the original Band Aid single and Live Aid concert took place to send famine relief). She went into Eritrea and Tigray, the provinces worst-affected by the drought, and at a London press conference immediately after leaving Ethiopia, she spoke with great feeling about the problems and the needs she had witnessed first-hand. She said: "If people are still interested in me, if my name makes them listen to what I want to say, then that is wonderful.

ABOVE and OVER PAGE: Audrey in Ethiopia. *UNICEF/Hulton Archive/Getty Images (2)*

But I am not interested in promoting Audrey Hepburn these days. I am interested in telling the world about how they can help in Ethiopia, and why I came away feeling optimistic … I went with so many people telling me how harrowing and dreadful it would be to see the extent of the suffering, the death and the despair. Certainly, I saw children in an advanced state of malnutrition, although they are not dying in masses as happened before. But I also witnessed how much is being done to help and how just a small amount of aid can assist in treating the sick, irrigating the land and planting new crops. I came to realize that Ethiopia's problems are not insoluble if only the world will give a little more." It was the first

of many interviews and meetings with the press, which took place during the next few weeks. She undertook a schedule that included as many as fifteen print and broadcast interviews a day, in Canada, Switzerland, Finland, Germany, Italy and the United States including breakfast with members of the U.S. Congress. "They were charming," she said later. "It was not easy to field some very difficult, unexpected questions about Ethiopia, dealing with the political situation, over coffee and grapefruit—but I was very gratified to hear that after this meeting the United States had augmented funds for Ethiopia."

On April 23–26, 1988, she represented UNICEF at

the International Children's Day celebration in Turkey, where she said: "Recently visiting Ethiopia I saw the faces of children—faces of pain and suffering and despair. But here we are surrounded by so many young lives full of health and happiness—and energy, which is indeed the greatest reward for all those who unite to work for a better world and for a happier childhood."

In October she visited UNICEF-assisted programs in Venezuela (15–18) and Ecuador (19–29). In February 1989, she visited Guatemala (5–6), Honduras (7–8), and El Salvador (9–11) where she launched the 1989 State of the World's Children Report; she then went to Mexico.

On her return, in April 1989, she was invited to testify at hearings of the House Foreign Operations Sub-Committee and the House Select Sub-Committee on Hunger. She also met President and Mrs. Bush at The White House. Shortly after she left for the Sudan to witness Operation Lifeline Sudan (April 12–16). She traveled to the rebel-held Southern Sudan, where she met with rebel leaders and witnessed the plight of the displaced in the Sudan.

Audrey went on to be of great assistance to fund-raising and advocacy efforts of a number of UNICEF National Committees including Ireland, Italy, the U.K., and France. In addition, in 1988, 1989, and 1990, she and Gregory Peck served as hosts for the "Danny Kaye Awards Show" telecast from the Netherlands throughout Europe. In November 1988, she starred in "Gift of Song," a televised concert from Vancouver benefiting the Canadian Committee; and in April spoke about UNICEF at the Empire Club Luncheon in Toronto.

"There is no deficit in human resources, only a deficit in human will, " she said in April 1989 at the National Press Club, Washington, D.C. "We cannot envisage a world of peace and compassion until children are no longer suffering from disease or are mutilated and neglected. Children cannot wait until the debt

crisis passes, we must help them now." In September she spoke at the UN Ambassador's Dinner in New York; in November she spoke at the Institute of Human Understanding dinner in New Orleans and in October 1989 she completed an extensive UNICEF mission that took her to Australia, Thailand, and Bangladesh where in various locations she visited UNICEF-assisted projects.

In March 1990, it was back to fund raising in the U.S. She went to Philadelphia, Houston, Chicago, and New York appearing with the New World Symphony, and was honored at a dinner by the Washington D.C. Advisory Council. September 30 found her an active

ABOVE: Audrey at a UNICEF press conference in New York City on March 23, 1988, after her first mission. *WireImage/Getty Images*

participant at the World Summit for Children, giving a series of press and broadcast interviews. Australia and New Zealand welcomed her in November 1990 for a series of events; she then traveled to Vietnam. She said, "They lack, of course. The school lacks books, which UNICEF is going to provide. They lack medicine, which UNICEF is providing. But the infrastructure is there. The extraordinary thing about Vietnam and its people, unlike some of our countries … There may be a deficit of resources but not of will. That is not always true about our country. We have the resources but not always enough human will."

For the December launch of the 1991 State of the World's Children Report she was again in New York, taking a major role through media interviews.

During 1992, though ill with the abdominal pains that would turn out to be the cancer that killed her, she continued her work for UNICEF, traveling to Somalia, Kenya, the United Kingdom, Switzerland, France and the United States. In October 1992—only days before she went to hospital—in Nairobi, after returning from Somalia, she passionately outlined to a gathering of 25 media representatives the problems she saw there, once again alluding to her childhood: "Unfortunately, it is too late for many children and mothers, but for many more there is still time. I speak from my own experience in Holland after WWII. I, along with hundreds of thousands, waited and struggled through five years of repression, violence, concentration camps, horrors, and starvation. I survived those five years—many others did not—but those who survived never lost hope. And in the proud eyes of the Somalis I spoke to, I saw that same hope. "

She summed up her view of UNICEF in March 1988: "I have seen not only the work of the United Nations, but of nations united to overcome the crisis. Long-term development aid, so little at present, must be increased. UNICEF has a wonderful long arm, trying to reach the most wounded, and UNICEF works in a marvelous way to help people retain their dignity. Given a spade, which UNICEF provides, they can dig a well. We must now make sure that they do not have to dig graves for their children."

LEFT: Audrey Hepburn launching the Supermarket Campaign for UNICEF, July 1989. *Mirrorpix*

RIGHT: First Lady Barbara Bush chats with Audrey during tea at the White House, April 7, 1989. *Bettmann/Corbis*

7

AUDREY'S LEGACY

"I decided, very early on, just to accept life unconditionally; I never expected it to do anything special for me, yet I seemed to accomplish far more than I had ever hoped. Most of the time it just happened to me without my ever seeking it."

Audrey Hepburn

The legacy Audrey Hepburn left behind her is an imperishable one. She embodied a look that would never age and her innocent, doe-eyed appearance, so much in contrast to the blonde, busty movie-queen stereotype of the time, continues to beguile. Her link with fashion designer Givenchy added the touch of class with which she is forever associated: Hepburn was only one of two people to wear the Tiffany Diamond, but in truth sparkled in any setting.

While her filmography is comparatively modest, Audrey Hepburn brought star quality to every role she undertook, and there's little doubt

that *Breakfast At Tiffany's* and *My Fair Lady* alone would have been enough to write her name large in Hollywood's hall of fame.

After the thrill of stardom faded she chose to use her fame for good, directing the camera lenses so long trained at her at the heartbreak caused by war and famine. There was no doubt her difficult and fatherless childhood in war-torn Europe had equipped her for the role, and it was one she fulfilled with a passion rarely seen on screen. "The 'Third World' is a term I don't like very much," she said, "because we're all one world. I want people to know that the largest part of humanity is suffering."

A movie star whose chic exterior disguised a big, big heart, Audrey Hepburn will never be forgotten.

LEFT and PREVIOUS PAGE: Audrey's white oak coffin was carried to the grave by the men in her life: her brother, her two sons, her second husband, her partner Robert Wolders, and her friend of forty years, Hubert de Givenchy. *Pascal Le Segretain/ Sygma/Corbis*

ABOVE: Sean (R) and Luca (L) pose for photographers during the presentation of the exhibition "Audrey in Rome," October 3, 2011. The exhibition ran from October 26 to December 4, 2011, at Rome's Ara Pacis Museum. *EPA/Guido Montani/Corbis*

RIGHT: French novelist and philanthropist Dominique Lapierre and his wife during their visit to an educational center in Keoradanga, south of Kolkata, February 28, 2007. Some $800,000 from the auction of Audrey's *Breakfast at Tiffany's* gown was donated to build fifteen schools for destitute Indian children. *Parth Sanyal/Reuters/Corbis*

ABOVE: Visitors look at the photographs displayed for "Audrey in Rome." *EPA/ Claudio Peri/Corbis*

LEFT: A wax figure of Audrey was unveiled at Madame Tussauds Hong Kong on September 27, 2011. *Xinhua/Chen Xiaowei/ Corbis*

RIGHT: Audrey has appeared on a number of stamps. A set of ten from a canceled 2001 German postal service campaign sold for $606,000, in October 2010, the funds going toward Audrey's Children's Fund and UNICEF Germany. *EPA/Roland Weihrach*

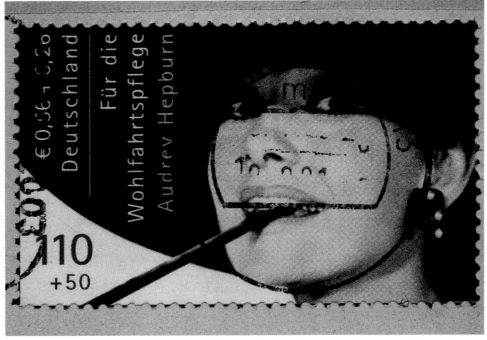

AUDREY'S AWARDS

"I've been lucky. Opportunities don't often come along. So, when they do, you have to grab them." Audrey Hepburn

1952

Best Debut Performance by an Actress for *Gigi*. The *Billboard* Annual Donaldson Award for Outstanding Achievement in Theatre, 1952.

Theatre World Award: Promising Personalities of the 1951–1952, Theatre Season for *Gigi*. *Theatre World*, 1952.

1953

Box Office Blue Ribbon Award for *Roman Holiday*, 1953.

1954

Academy Award: Oscar, Best Actress (1953) for *Roman Holiday*. Academy of Motion Pictures Arts and Science, 1954.

BAFTA Best Film Actress Award (1953) for *Roman Holiday*. British Academy of Film and Television Arts, 1954.

Golden Globe Award: Best Motion Picture Actress, Drama (1953) for *Roman Holiday*. Hollywood Foreign Press Association, 1954.

Look Award, Actress of the Year (1953). Presented by *Look* magazine on "Colgate Comedy Hour," NBC-TV, 1954.

NYFCC Best Actress Award (1953) for *Roman Holiday*. New York Film Critics Circle, 1954.

Tony Award: Best Dramatic Actress for *Ondine*. The American Theatre Wing and The League of American Theatres and Producers, 1954.

1955

Academy Award: Oscar Nomination, Best Actress (1954) for *Sabrina*.

BAFTA Best Film Actress Nomination (1954) for *Sabrina*.

Golden Globe Henrietta Award: World Film Favorite, Female.

NYFCC Best Actress Nomination (1954) for *Sabrina*.

Victoire du Cinéma Francais Award, 1955.

1956

Modern Screen Award: Best Performance for *War and Peace*, 1956.

1957

BAFTA Best Film Actress Nomination (1956) for *War and Peace*.

Golden Globe Nomination: Best Motion Picture Actress, Drama (1956) for *War and Peace*.

NYFCC Best Actress Nomination (1956) for *War and Peace*.

1958

Golden Globe Nomination: Best Motion Picture Actress, Musical/Comedy (1957) for *Love in the Afternoon*.

Golden Laurel Award: First Place, Top Female Comedy Performance for *Love in the Afternoon*, 1958.

NYFCC Best Actress Nomination (1957) for *Love in the Afternoon*.

1959

Best Film Actress of 1959. Variety Club of Great Britain, 1959.

Zulueta Prize: Best Actress for *The Nun's Story*. San Sebastian International Film Festival, 1959.

1960

Academy Award: Oscar Nomination, Best Actress for *The Nun's Story*.

Adam 'n' Eve Award. Motion Picture Costumers, 1960.

BAFTA Best Film Actress Award (1959) for *The Nun's Story*.

David di Donatello Best Foreign Actress Award for *The Nun's Story*. Accademia del Cinema Italiano, 1960.

Golden Globe Nomination: Best Motion Picture Actress, Drama (1959) for *The Nun's Story*.

Golden Laurel Award: Second Place, Top Female Dramatic Performance for *The Nun's Story*, 1960.

Hollywood Walk of Fame Star, Motion Picture Category.

NYFCC Best Actress Award (1959) for *The Nun's Story*.

1961

Cleveland Critics Circle Award: Best Actress. Cleveland Critics, 1961.

Golden Laurel Award Nomination: Top Female Star. 1961.

1962

Academy Awards: Oscar Nomination, Best Actress (1961) for *Breakfast at Tiffany's*.

David di Donatello Best Foreign Actress Award for *Breakfast at Tiffany's*.

Golden Globe Nomination: Best Motion Picture Actress, Musical/Comedy (1961) for *Breakfast at Tiffany's*.

Golden Laurel Award: Third Place, Top Female Comedy Performance for *Breakfast at Tiffany's*, 1962.

Golden Laurel Award Nomination: Top Female Dramatic Performance for *The Children's Hour*, 1962.

1963

Golden Laurel Award Nomination: Top Female Star. 1963.

1964

Golden Globe Nomination: Best Motion Picture Actress, Musical/ Comedy (1963) for *Charade*.
Golden Laurel Award: Third Place, Top Female Comedy Performance for *Charade*, 1964.
Victoire du Cinéma Francais Award. 1964.

1965

BAFTA Best Film Actress Award (1963) for *Charade*.
David di Donatello Best Foreign Actress Award for *My Fair Lady*.
Golden Globe Nomination: Best Motion Picture Actress, Musical/Comedy (1964) for *My Fair Lady*.
Golden Laurel Award: Third Place, Female Comedy Performance for *My Fair Lady*, 1965.
NYFCC Best Actress Award (1964) for *My Fair Lady*.

1966

Golden Laurel Award Nomination: Top Female Star. 1966.

1968

Academy Award: Oscar Nomination, Best Actress *Wait Until Dark*.
Golden Globe Nomination: Best Motion Picture Actress, Drama (1967) for *Wait Until Dark*.
Golden Globe Nomination: Best Motion Picture Actress, Musical/Comedy (1967) for *Two for the Road*.
Golden Laurel Award: Second Place, Top Female Star. 1968.

Golden Laurel Award: Third Place, Female Dramatic Performance for *Wait Until Dark*, 1968.
Maschera d'Argento Award: Achievement in the Arts. 1968.
Nastri D'Argento (Silver Ribbon Award). Italian National Syndicate of Film.
NYFCC Best Actress Award Nomination (1967) for *Wait Until Dark*.
Special Tony Award. The American Theatre Wing and The League of American Theatres and Producers, 1968.

1976

Variety Club of New York: Humanitarian Award for contributions to the world of motion pictures and charitable efforts on behalf of all children of all nations. Variety—The Children's Charity of New York, 1976.

1987

Commandeur de L'Ordre des Arts et des Lettres for significant contributions to furthering the arts in France and throughout the world. Presented by the French Minister of Culture and Communications, 1987.

1988

The International Danny Kaye Award for Children. Presented by the U.S. Committee for UNICEF, 1988.

1989

International Humanitarian Award. Presented for the first time in history by the Institute for Human Understanding, 1989. Prix d' Humanité Award, 1989.

1990

Cecil B. DeMille Award: Golden Globe Lifetime Achievement.

Children's Champion Award. Washington UNICEF Council, 1990.

Seventh Annual UNICEF Ball honoring Audrey Hepburn. UNICEF, 1990.

1991

Bambi Award. Berlin, Germany, 1991.

Certificate of Merit for UNICEF Ambassadorship. UNICEF "Acts of Consequence" Tour, 1991.

Champion of Children Award for work on behalf of the world's children. Children's Institute International, 1991.

Distinguished International Lifetime Award: Sigma Theta Tau International Audrey Hepburn Award named after Audrey, given to individuals in recognition for their international work on behalf of children. Sigma Theta Tau International Nursing Association, 1991.

Gala Tribute Honoree. Film Society of Lincoln Center, 1991.

Golden Plate Award for achievement in the arts and public service, "representing the many who excel in the great fields of endeavor." The American Academy of Achievement, 1991.

Humanitarian Award. Variety Clubs International, 1991.

Master Screen Artist. USA Film Festival, 1991.

"Sindaci per L' infanzia" (Mayors for Children) Award. UNICEF, 1991.

1992

Alan Shawn Feinstein World Hunger Awards: Honorary Chair and Speaker. For the prevention and reduction of world hunger. Brown University, 1992.

BAFTA Lifetime Achievement Award. British Academy of Film and Television Arts, 1992.

Gold Medal Award: Casita Maria Fiesta. Casita Maria, 1992.

George Eastman Award for distinguished contribution to the art of film. George Eastman House, 1992.

Lifetime of Style Award. Council of Fashion Designers of America, 1992.

Presidential Medal of Freedom Award for contributions to the árts and humanitarian work, 1992

1993

Emmy Award: Outstanding Individual Achievement.

Grammy Award: Best Spoken Word Album for Children for *Audrey Hepburn's Enchanted Tales*. The Recording Academy, 1993.

Jean Hersholt Humanitarian Award (1992). Oscar accepted by Sean H. Ferrer. Academy of Motion Pictures Arts and Science, 1993.

The Pearl S. Buck Woman's Award. The Pearl S. Buck Foundation, 1993.

SAG Lifetime Achievement Award. Screen Actors Guild of America, 1993.

2002

The Spirit of Audrey Hepburn. Unveiling of a bronze sculpture honoring Audrey entitled "The Spirit of Audrey," by sculptor John Kennedy, in the public plaza at UNICEF headquarters in New York, 2002.

2003

Legends of Hollywood, U.S. Postage Stamp. U.S. Postal Service, 2003.

Photography

The Publisher would like to thank Casper Kuijer for the photographs of Arnhem and Toby Hopkins and Sean Harry at Getty Images and David Scripps at Mirrorpix who helped with the photo research. Photographs are credited with the captions. The individual references are:

Corbis—pp2 JS2754, 5 U1066010, 7 42-18406265, 8 BE020141, 9 VV2134, 14 U1313921, 16 U2110789, 17 0000225153-007, 19 42-21929242, 23 U1199858, 24 HU005786, 45 U1007185, 46 BE029541, 47 U984296ACME, 53 BE059279, 56 HU015517, 57 PEN3795, 58 UKD3151AINP, 59 BE030816, 60 U1250528INP, 61 U1250750INP, 62 U1251085INP, 63 U1061095, 67 U1116135, 71 JS1568191, 74 42-20214693, 75 42-20214696, 76 BE030810, 78 U1251694INP, 79 BE057171, 80 SF33406, 81 42-15424542, 82 U1088881, 85 42-30064717, 86 U1322975INP, 87 42-20014427, 88 VV3304, 90 42-15424544, 93 SF36461, 94 0000340135-001, 95 U1147775A, 96 BE057163, 97 0000356967-003, 98 U1444919, 99 AABE001068, 100 0000304599-013, 113 U1551944, 116 U1239975, 117 U1619871-6, 119 U1221150, 120 U1177979A, 121 BE031863, 122 42-19501978, 124 42-30064856, 125 42-30064859, 126 JS1566885, 127 JS1566886, 130 BE025157, 129 42-26111688, 133 E9676, 134 42-15424549, 138 U1592081, 140 U1700357, 143 AX020914, 144 U1862256, 146 U1962080, 148 BE020938, 151 BE020888, 152 AX020909, 153 AX020917, 154 42-26596977, 157 42-27392592, 160 OUT012151, 161 VE003134, 162 42-27903547, 164 0000278003-002, 166 42-16732673, 167 0000267264-013, 168 42-22482069, 169 42-25506992, 170 SF9154, 177 U90047083-7, 178 0000282391-013, 180 0000282391-027, 182 42-29952868, 42-17986739, 184 42-29704171, 185T 42-30436914, 185B 42-22275646, 187 BE030823, 188 KV004614

Getty—pp1 79025559, 4 89740662, 11 134204146, 21 78953363, 27 1652368, 29 78979820, 30 92607942, 31 92607932, 35 3360716, 36 79040864, 38 3134977, 39 3092867, 40 98166554, 41 78951453, 42 78979817, 43 78950449, 48 79040552, 49, 79045498, 51 3248351, 52 78988237, 65 73908880, 66 107350171, 72 3062507, 77 73909192, 84 132706447, 92 79023890, 102 1944736, 108 82138887, 115 89726712, 118 3206062, 123 56481755, 128 119107346, 131 78951466, 132 107154572, 136 108886843, 137 89726761, 139 109253090, 141 50587691, 142 105188223, 147 106755799, 150 89726752, 151 89726755, 151 inset 130238423, 165 110134660, 173 89726706, 174 89726764, 175 105813204, 190 89438722, 191T 137471960, 191B 85246969

Mirrorpix—pp13 00048191, 32 00138689, 33 00145671, 34 00279772, 37 00146051, 44 00140855, 54 00285327, 55 00285115, 68L 00145738, 68R 00146514, 69 00055528, 70 00048033, 73 00086708, 83 00138553, 103 00279773, 104 00140724, 105 00140518, 106 00149700, 107 00145690, 109 00279782, 110 00279775, 111 00279776, 112 00158550, 114 00146365, 158 00193227, 176 00162101